A GREAT
STATE FAIR

ALSO BY WILLIAM B. FRIEDRICKS

A GREAT STATE FAIR

The Blue Ribbon Foundation and the Revival of the Iowa State Fair

WILLIAM B. FRIEDRICKS

Business Publications Corporation Inc.

A Great State Fair:
The Blue Ribbon Foundation and Revival of the Iowa State Fair
is published by Business Publications Corporation Inc., an
Iowa corporation.

Cover photo by Mark Iwig.

ISBN-978-0-9965213-4-5
Library of Congress Control Number: 2017909576
Business Publications Corporation, Des Moines, Iowa

Business Publications Corporation Inc.
The Depot at Fourth
100 4th Street
Des Moines, Iowa 50309
(515) 288-3336

For Jackie

CONTENTS

Photographs appear following pages 46 and 103.

ACKNOWLEDGMENTS

Over the past fifteen years or so, there have been several books published on the Iowa State Fair. Mary Kay Shanley's *Our State Fair: Iowa's Blue Ribbon Story* (2000) offered a richly illustrated popular history of the fair; Thomas Leslie's *Iowa State Fair: Country Comes to Town* (2007) provided a brief narrative focused on the fair's buildings and layout of the grounds; and Don Greiman, with Jane Cox, in *A Blue Ribbon Life: Memories of the Iowa State Fair* (2012), gave us recollections of the exhibition from a longtime member of the Fair Board. More recently, Kurt Ullrich's *The Iowa State Fair* (2014) captured the essence of the fair with photographs and short essays; while Chris Rasmussen's *Carnival in the Countryside: The History of the Iowa State Fair* (2015) afforded us the first scholarly treatment of the fair.

This study presents a different perspective. In 2015, I was recruited to write the history of the Iowa State Fair Blue Ribbon Foundation, the fundraising entity responsible for raising millions of dollars and saving the crumbling Iowa State Fairgrounds. The foundation's accomplishments are truly remarkable, but the only way to understand their significance is to put the story in the context of the fair's long and sometimes difficult history. Once hired for the project, I was left alone, free to interpret the available sources and write the narrative as I saw fit.

Many at the Iowa State Fair and the Blue Ribbon Foundation provided assistance as the project progressed. John Putney, the foundation's first director, met with me many times, answered numerous questions, and opened his personal papers and photographs to me. Current executive director Peter Cownie and assistant director Robin Taylor were quite accommodating, while Cindy Lundeen at the Iowa State Fair and Drew Norton and Gina Rooney of the Blue Ribbon Foundation were helpful as well. Iowa State Fair manager and CEO Gary Slater and the fair's senior plant operations director Scott Worth offered important insights, as did former and current Fair Board members Don Greiman, Jerry Parkin, Bob Schlutz, and Paul Vaassen. Beth (Reinig) Greiner, the foundation's first staffer, graciously loaned me an important collection of her personal papers. And although he did not work for the fair or foundation, Rox Laird deserves special mention. As a *Des Moines Register* editorial writer, Laird kept close tabs on the fair, shined a spotlight on its problems, and cheered on the work of the Blue Ribbon Foundation. He gave me access to his files on the fair, which proved essential to this study. Thank you, Rox, Beth, and all at the fair and Blue Ribbon Foundation.

Local historian John Zeller has been helpful to me over the years, and once again, he shared his meticulous research notes. I'm not sure how historians could write about central Iowa's past without John's assistance. Susan Knapp, a key supporter of the fair, kindly loaned me her blue ribbon necklace to be photographed for the book. And a number of others sat for interviews, talked with me on the phone, or shared their papers with me. I could not have completed this history without their help. A list of these individuals is included at the end of the book.

I am grateful to Linda Sinclair, Allie Walker, Britney Samuelson, and Ashtyne Madsen at Iowa History Center at Simpson College who made the interviews much more user friendly by transcribing them for me. Once again, it was a pleasure to work with the fine staff at Business Publications Corporation. Thank you to Ashley Holter and Catherine Skepnek, who oversaw the project, Renee Johnson, whose close reading and editing skills improved the manuscript, Duane Tinkey, who took some photographs for me, and Lauren Hayes, who designed the book.

Of course, my family deserves special thanks. My dad, Burt Friedricks, my in-laws, Jerry and Wynona Crawford, and my daughters, Sarah and Emily, offered constant encouragement. Most important was my wife, Jackie. She is always my first and last reader, making everything I write better. Her love, laughter, and dear friendship have sustained me since we first met. That year, she introduced this Southern Californian to the Iowa State Fair, and treks there have become annual summer events for us. For acquainting me with the fair and everything else, I dedicate this book to her, with love.

A GREAT
STATE
FAIR

INTRODUCTION

As they have done for over 160 years, Iowans gather each summer for their annual celebration called the Iowa State Fair. The state's cultural treasure is at once an educational forum, livestock show, amusement park, food competition, concert venue, 4-H convention, racecar track, outdoor restaurant, talent contest, implement dealer, and living history museum, which every year recounts the Iowa experience. A million people pour through the gates every August to be part of this quintessential American exhibition, made famous by Phil Stong's popular book *State Fair* and the film and theatrical versions that followed. The Iowa State Fair is, in the words of historian Chris Rasmussen, "Iowa's central institution, event and symbol. New Jersey has the Shore. Kentucky has the Derby. Iowa has the fair." And of course a major part of the fair's allure is the picturesque, park-like fairground, with its well-preserved exposition-style buildings standing proudly next to the gleaming new brick facilities that complement these graceful historic structures.[1]

In recent years the national media has been singing the Iowa State Fair's praises. The *Wall Street Journal* called it the "classic" state fair; the best-selling travel book *1,000 Places to See Before You Die* featured it as the only state fair on the list; and *Midwest Living* magazine includes the Iowa State Fair among its "Thirty Things Every Midwesterner Should Experience."[2]

This grand success was anything but inevitable, however. The fair was created by the Iowa State Agricultural Society (ISAS), a private entity, in the mid-nineteenth century and started as an itinerant exhibition that traveled every couple of years to and from the larger towns in eastern Iowa. Funding was always a problem, and even after the ISAS began receiving legislative subsidies for the fair, it still struggled. When public aid ended, the situation became dire—until the fair moved to Des Moines in the late 1870s. Once located in the state's rapidly growing capital, the fair's future seemed bright. It would remain in Des Moines, where a permanent fairgrounds was established in the 1880s, but the fair's financial problems continued until 1900, when the ISAS and the fair were taken over by a new state agency, the Iowa Department of Agriculture. Although now under the auspices of the state, the fair was intended to run as a self-sustaining institution, with operating expenses and maintenance paid out of fair receipts except in cases where the legislature granted special appropriations.

Such special funding was soon forthcoming for new facilities, opening a golden age for the fair. During the first two decades of the twentieth century, many of the Beaux-Arts-inspired buildings that added grandeur and dignity to the grounds—the Livestock Pavilion, the Agriculture Building, the Administration Building, the Grandstand, and the Varied Industries Building, as well as the livestock barns—were erected. But decades passed, times changed, and Iowa's rural population fell by half. By the 1960s, the agricultural-based Iowa State Fair, though quaint, seemed passé to the increasing number of Iowans who were growing further and further removed from the farm. At the same time, the once stately buildings that adorned the fairgrounds were becoming more expensive to maintain and inadequate for present needs.

The Fair Board, managers, and staff sought solutions to turn the fair around. Task forces were formed, consultants hired, and studies conducted. New marketing plans and a greater focus on entertainment led to a rebound in attendance, but with no funding for renovation, the buildings continued to deteriorate. There was serious talk of abandoning the current fairgrounds and building a new one, but the plans went nowhere. Pari-mutuel horse racing was introduced in hopes of providing sorely needed funding, but the few seasons the ponies ran failed to deliver the expected big payoff.

Symbolic of the fairgrounds' sad state of affairs was the 1980 demolition of the dilapidated Women's and Children's Building. Erected in 1914, the popular structure had to be taken down because the Fair

Board lacked the $700,000 necessary to restore it. Several years later, a study suggested just how shabby the fair had become, estimating that $32 million were required to renovate and rebuild the fairgrounds. In desperation, fair manager Marion Lucas and the Fair Board decided on a new approach: develop a foundation devoted solely to raising money for the fair and fairgrounds.

As the board worked to create such a foundation, the *Des Moines Register* weighed in on the matter. Over the years, the newspaper had been an important advocate for the fair and beginning in 1991, intensified its campaign with editorial writer Rox Laird addressing the abysmal state of the fair's facilities. That summer, he opened the discussion with a sharp op-ed piece that shone light on the derelict fairgrounds, which he said, "was crumbling at the joints." He called on Iowans to step up, laying out a game plan that suggested "a major capital-improvement program... financed through a combination of public and private money."[3]

Several months after Laird's essay, the Fair Board's new fund-raising arm, the Iowa State Fair Blue Ribbon Foundation, was up and running. After a slow first year, the Blue Ribbon Foundation found its footing in 1993 and was relaunched under the direction of John Putney, a cattleman and former aide to US Senator Chuck Grassley. Putney's connections, affability, and longtime passion for the Iowa State Fair made him the perfect hire. He considered the fair a vital part of Iowa's heritage and culture and saw the fairgrounds as an essential component to the fair experience. Most important, Putney was able to communicate these feelings to Iowans of all stripes, and his message struck a chord.

Once hired, Putney moved quickly. He and his small foundation staff—initially one, which would ultimately grow to three—focused on the fair's significance and the urgent need to restore the fairgrounds. They successfully pursued corporate support and created a variety of giving programs, making it easy for Iowans of all socioeconomic groups to support what Putney always reminded them was "their fair." The foundation sold bottled water at the fair; created the annual Corndog Kickoff, a benefit auction; and developed sponsorship programs that allowed fairgoers "to acquire" their own piece of the fair by buying brick pavers, trees, lamps, or benches spread throughout the fairgrounds. Giving to the fair was made even easier through the

Corndog Checkoff, which allowed Iowans to contribute through their state income tax forms.

Early on in this fund-raising effort, the most touching gift came from a homeless woman who had seen a poster touting the Corndog Checkoff as a simple way to give to the fair. After explaining that she wanted to support the fair but would not be filing taxes that year, she gave $1 in quarters to the cause.[4]

Putney also worked the other end of the spectrum by courting big donors. Key here was Bill Knapp, a well-heeled Des Moines real estate developer and philanthropist, who Putney won over in 1997, when he gave $1 million toward the fair's restoration. Knapp would go on to contribute another $1.5 million, but more significantly, he became a champion for the cause, encouraging wealthy friends and colleagues to open their wallets, resulting in millions more for the Blue Ribbon Foundation.

Another component critical to the effort was getting legislative support, something fair officials had failed to do in recent years. The politically savvy Putney immediately went after public money, persuading state representatives and senators that like the regent universities, the Iowa State Fair was state-owned and merited legislative support. His lobbying paid off that first year, and the statehouse coffers were opened for the fairgrounds' restoration.

Of course, Putney and the foundation did not encounter steady success. There were problems and setbacks as well as squabbles with fair management as the foundation's roles and responsibilities were ironed out, but Putney and his team swiftly won the much-needed support and buy-in from individuals, corporations, and legislators. As a result, the foundation blew past fund-raising goals, besting the rosiest predictions. By 2003, the Blue Ribbon Foundation had amassed $53.5 million for the fair, a whopping 75 percent more than the $30 million, ten-year goal established in 1993.

Such funding ushered in a remarkable revival for the Iowa State Fair. The rebuilding of the run-down fairgrounds coincided with the foundation's existence, and in ten years, the transformation was nearly complete. In August 2003, the *Des Moines Register* explained, "Almost every structure on the 425-acre grounds has been remodeled or renovated in the past decade. From the installation of air conditioning in the Varied

Industries Building to the reconstruction of the popular Ye Old Mill, the fair has benefited from a makeover unprecedented in its 149-year history." The Iowa State Fairgrounds was again a showplace, now of beautifully restored historic buildings. Dignity had been returned to the stately, century-old structures that had defined Iowa's annual summer celebration for decades.[5]

As others in the fair industry looked on with envy at the turnaround in Des Moines, the Iowa State Fair Board and new manager Gary Slater now had the luxury of thinking strategically about fairground additions designed to keep the exhibition vibrant and relevant. To that end, new structures such as the Paul R. Knapp Animal Learning Center and the Richard O. Jacobson Exhibition Center went up, bankrolled by the foundation.

Today the Iowa State Fair is thriving. Its fabled but once derelict fairgrounds have been restored and now expanded thanks to the Blue Ribbon Foundation, which to date has raised $135 million. In 2014, after twenty-one years at the foundation's helm, Putney stepped down in favor of Peter Cownie. The Fair Board looked to Cownie to build on the foundation's great success and bring in a new generation of donors. Early indicators suggest he is doing just that. Currently, Cownie and the foundation are working with Slater, the Fair Board, and staff on the fair's biggest capital improvement project in history as together they strive to promote, preserve, and improve this proud Iowa tradition well into the twenty-first century.

PRELUDE TO A
PERMANENT FAIRGROUNDS

Before it had a permanent facility and long before there was a need for the Iowa State Fair Blue Ribbon Foundation, the Iowa State Fair had enjoyed a long history. Much like other Midwestern state fairs, the Iowa institution had its origins in the 1850s, growing out of an agricultural fair movement begun several decades earlier in western Massachusetts. The annual gatherings were sponsored by local agricultural societies to disseminate new agricultural techniques as well as showcase prize livestock, crops, and home manufactures in competitive exhibitions.[1]

The fair movement spread as Americans pushed westward. Once Iowa was opened for settlement in 1833, it became a preferred destination as travel guides such as *Galland's Iowa Emigrant* lured pioneers by touting its "fertile soil…pure atmosphere, and excellent water." With few natural impediments, settlement of Iowa proceeded rapidly over the next thirty years, moving from southeast to northwest. By the time Iowa achieved statehood in 1846, its population stood at ninety-six thousand and rose to over one million by 1870.[2]

Most heading to Iowa came from farming backgrounds, and much like settlers in the region's other territories and states, they soon established county fairs. The Iowa Territorial Legislature, in fact, promoted such activity by passing a series of laws allowing for the incorporation of agricultural societies and promising state financial support. After a false start in Van Buren County, several other Iowa counties organized agricultural societies in the early 1850s. In 1853, the Jefferson County Agricultural Society called for the creation of a state fair by inviting representatives of all state county agricultural societies to a convention to establish a state fair.[3]

Only five counties sent representatives to the Fairfield (Jefferson County's seat) convention, but the small group pushed ahead. To oversee a state fair, it established the Iowa State Agricultural Society (ISAS) for "the promotion of agriculture, horticulture, manufactures, mechanics, and household arts." As might be expected, the newly minted ISAS chose Fairfield for the first annual Iowa State Fair, scheduled for the following October 1854.[4]

The fairgrounds were laid out on six acres, surrounded by a ten-foot-high fence. Inside, a 250-foot-long shed along the north side of the enclosure was built for exhibits, while livestock pens and stalls were situated along the rest of the perimeter. A quarter-mile track sat in the interior, with a viewing stand for dignitaries, speakers, and fair officials located in the infield. Estimates of the fair's opening day crowd ranged from seven thousand to ten thousand people, roughly seven to ten times the population of the host town. The throng of people, "the largest gathering in the history of the frontier state," according to historian Chris Rasmussen, listened to speeches by fair officials and agricultural experts, saw samples of Iowa's best livestock, crops, and domestic manufactures, learned about the latest in plows, planters, and other agricultural implements, and enjoyed entertainments including equestrian events featuring women riders.[5]

Although the fair appeared to be a great success, it lost money, partly because a number of counterfeit bills were accepted at the gate. But attorney Thomas W. Clagett, president of the ISAS, was especially enthusiastic about the fair and personally made up the deficit. He and the society remained optimistic and planned an even bigger fair for the following year. The 1855 fair was again held in Fairfield and exceeded the society's high hopes. Its success set the stage for making the exhibition an annual event. As Joshua M. Shaffer, the society secretary and manager of the fair, noted, "The First Fair was an experiment," but the second fair demonstrated, "that a State Society for the Promotion of Agriculture and Mechanics can and will be sustained by the people of Iowa."[6]

After this second fair, two important changes were in the offing. First, ISAS leaders thought it important to move the annual event to a new location every couple of years. Their thinking reflected Iowa's primitive transportation infrastructure. With poor roads and only the beginning of a railroad network, inland travel throughout the state was difficult. As a result, few beyond Jefferson County's local population attended the Fairfield-hosted fairs and still fewer were willing to bring their livestock great distances to exhibit.[7]

Thus, ISAS officials thought, they should take the fair to the people, moving it between Iowa's regional population centers, then almost entirely in the eastern half of the state. Besides reaching out to new patrons every few years, the itinerant fair also brought a huge boost to local economies wherever it was staged, pleasing area business owners and merchants. The possibility of this cash infusion led to intense competitions between cities seeking to host the annual exposition. After its first two years in Fairfield, the fair was held in eight eastern Iowa cities—Muscatine, Oskaloosa, Iowa City, Dubuque, Burlington, Clinton, Keokuk, and Cedar Rapids— before moving to Des Moines in 1879.

More important was a change in funding. The ISAS was originally established as a private corporation and relied entirely on monies it raised, most of which came from membership dues, donations, and any revenue generated from the Iowa State Fair. But from its inception, the organization's leaders argued that because the society served Iowa's citizenry broadly and promoted economic growth across the state, it merited public funding from the legislature. By early 1857, lawmakers agreed and passed an act ensuring the society an annual appropriation of $2,000. The statute required the society to provide an annual report spelling out its activities and an analysis of Iowa agriculture over the past year.[8]

State financial assistance proved important, getting the fair through lean years of depression during the late 1850s and helping to sustain the institution through the Civil War, when society officials held the exposition despite the conflict. By the end of hostilities in 1865, the size of the fair had grown five times since its founding, occupying a thirty-acre site in Burlington, and included "the largest indoor halls" yet for exhibits and a half-mile horse track "surrounded by an amphitheater with seating for 3,000."[9]

It looked like the ISAS had a winning formula. The fair was growing, and receipts were up. But there were problems. Complaints rose about holding the fair in certain locations, and moving the event from town to town was expensive. Even though the Iowa State Fair was usually held on county fairgrounds, such facilities usually required updating and expansion.

Fortunately for the society, business leaders soon understood the positive economic impact the fair brought and shouldered much of these costs.

Unfortunately, just as the ISAS had enjoyed three years of very successful fairs in Cedar Rapids (1871–73), state aid for the fair was ended following the onset of the depression of 1873. This raised serious financial concerns for the society, and by mid-decade, it was near bankruptcy.[10]

Amid these troubles, Iowa was growing. From 1860 to 1880, its population rose two-and-a-half times, climbing to 1.65 million while settlement was increasingly pushing into the central and western regions of the state. Understandably, there were calls for the fair to move west as well, and many looked to Des Moines to host the exhibition.

When the fair began in 1854, Fort Des Moines (the name would be changed to Des Moines in 1857) was little more than a frontier outpost of less than 1,500 people. But the seeds of change were being sown. A year earlier, the town benefited from the federal government decision to set up a land office there. The office sold newly opened Iowa land for $1.25 per acre, bringing thousands through the community. More important for the long term was the city's central location, which in 1855 earned it the prized designation of state capital.[11]

It was this central location and the arrival of the railroads that took advantage of it that transformed Des Moines. From the 1860s on, city business leaders worked to connect Des Moines with the outside world. To that point, residents had depended on erratic riverboat service and stage lines. By 1866, the city welcomed the Des Moines Valley Railroad, the first to enter Des Moines, linking it to Keokuk and the eastern United States. More important, however, was the arrival of the Chicago, Rock Island & Pacific Railroad (Rock Island) in 1867, which connected the city directly to Chicago and the national rail network.[12]

As Des Moines's ascendance became apparent, interest mounted for locating the fair in the city. The increasingly influential Republican *Iowa State Register* (eventually renamed the *Des Moines Register*) began suggesting Des Moines as a site for the Iowa State Fair as early as 1870, and its advocacy picked up as the decade unfolded. In November 1874, a group of western and central Iowa businessmen founded the Iowa Agricultural and Mechanical Association to lobby the ISAS for such a move. The *Register* supported their effort, writing, "Des Moines is central. Six railroads center here, reaching out routes for easy transportation to every part of the State. Heretofore Western and Central Iowa have been practically debarred from participation in this gathering of the Hawkeye farmers. With the Fair here, all parts of the State would be equally accessible to it." Even though the Democratic *Des Moines Leader* also backed the cause, fair secretary John Shaffer was not persuaded and remained committed to the fair traveling throughout eastern Iowa.[13]

Boosters continued building and nurturing Des Moines, and by 1881, nine railroads entered the city; by 1884, it was fourteen, with thirty-eight daily passenger trains running in and out of the community. Now clearly the transportation center of the state, Des Moines was on its way to being the commercial center as well. And with an 1880 population at 22,400, the city had become the largest in Iowa.[14]

This reality and the promotional efforts of Des Moines civic leaders finally pushed the ISAS to move the fair to the city in 1879. The fairgrounds were constructed on sixty acres of land owned by attorney Tallmadge E. Brown (known as Brown's Park) situated west of the downtown between Center Street and Grand Avenue, and Thirty-Eighth and Forty-Second Streets. Today's Ingersoll Avenue runs through what would have been the middle of the site. As had been done with all previous fairs, a high fence was erected around the grounds, which, when the fair opened in the beginning of September, included five hastily erected large halls for offices and exhibitions, a dining hall, an amphitheater with seating for six thousand, livestock pens and stalls, and a race track. The Rock Island Railroad built a special spur line to the grounds.[15]

Fair attendance topped one hundred thousand, and Shaffer believed the location of Des Moines was instrumental to the record-setting fair. Other cities throughout the state would continue to compete for the fair, but this success in Des Moines, together with the city's growing population and central location, seemed to make keeping the exhibition in the capital a foregone conclusion.[16]

The fair grew over the next few years, and society leadership decided a permanent fairground was needed to solidify the fair's reputation and success. One official explained that the itinerant nature of the fair moving "like a traveling circus" was detrimental to the exhibition's image. In 1884, the ISAS requested a $100,000 appropriation from the state legislature for the acquisition of a permanent fairground. Lawmakers responded by allocating $50,000 if the society could raise $50,000 to purchase such a site.[17]

Again, several Iowa cities jockeyed for the fair, but Des Moines was clearly the frontrunner. It had benefitted handsomely from hosting the fair over the past five years and was unwilling to surrender the annual event. Led by merchant Isaac Brandt, the Des Moines business community stepped forward with an open wallet. Key donors included real estate, insurance, and railroad entrepreneurs F. M. Hubbell and his partner, Jefferson Scott Polk, who assisted with the fund-raising campaign and gave $2,000 to the cause. Railroad companies, which saw a Des Moines fair as good for their bottom line, contributed generously as well.[18]

Within months, Des Moines had raised more than the requisite $50,000 and turned the money over to the society, which, in the spring of 1885, purchased the Calvin Thornton farm for the permanent fairgrounds. The 266-acre parcel sat two miles east of the state capitol and was bounded by University and Dean Avenues on the north and south and stretched from East Thirtieth to East Thirty-Sixth Streets from east to west. Then, as per the legislation that provided public funds for the acquisition, the society deeded the land to the state, which in turn granted the society use of the site for the fair.[19]

The purchase of a permanent fairground in Des Moines closed an era for the Iowa State Fair. For thirty years, the ISAS had built and developed the annual fair into a respected institution, growing it from a small and relatively local exhibition traveling among eastern Iowa cities every few years toward a true statewide event held in the capital city. Along the way, the ISAS's status as a private corporation became somewhat murky. Early on, its leaders successfully lobbied the legislature for annual funding, arguing that the society and its fair advanced agriculture and the general economy of the state. This made the society something of a quasi-government agency, but after nearly twenty years, lawmakers ended the subsidy, forcing the society to fend for itself.[20]

Now the society was banking on the new fairgrounds to sustain and expand the exhibition. Financial issues persisted, however, and the question remained whether or not a private corporation could or should shoulder the responsibility for the Iowa State Fair.

SOMETHING WORTH SAVING

If moving the Iowa State Fair to Des Moines reinvigorated the exhibition, establishing and then developing the permanent fairgrounds in the city was critical to making the annual event a fixture of Iowa culture. Over the next few decades, fair officials balanced short-term needs with long-term planning as they went about designing and building the Iowa State Fairgrounds. There were difficulties along the way, but once the fair became a creature of state government, the modern fairgrounds took shape, and save for a handful of structures that have come down or been erected since, fairgoers today would both recognize and feel comfortable amid the grand structures and landscaped grounds that were memorialized in 1932 by Phil Stong's best-selling book *State Fair*.

Once the Calvin Thornton farm was acquired in June 1885, the Iowa State Agriculture Society (ISAS) board created a committee charged with touring other fairgrounds to glean ideas that might prove useful for their facility. Members visited several sites, including the Chicago Driving Park, the grounds of the Saint Louis Exposition in Missouri, and the new Minnesota State Fairgrounds in Saint Paul. Maybe most helpful was their finding in Saint Louis, where they noted that the "general exhibition buildings are not costly but are substantially built." This information certainly must have been well received, because many on the board hoped that the construction of impressive buildings on the fairgrounds would elevate the agricultural exposition and hopefully lessen the need for various entertainments. And because their budget was tight, board members would have been pleased to learn that such structures could be erected with limited funds.[1]

To ensure the fairgrounds were laid out in a sensible, orderly manner, the board retained Jacob Weidenmann, a highly regarded New York City landscape architect, to prepare plans for the fairgrounds. Weidenmann was already well-known in Des Moines; he had recently designed the grounds of the Iowa State Capitol as well as prepared a subdivision for businessmen Jefferson Scott Polk and F. M. Hubbell on property adjacent to Terrace Hill (now the governor's mansion) that Hubbell had acquired in 1884. Weidenmann's initial impressions of the Thornton farm were favorable: "The grounds contain everything which it is possible to have to make first-class fair grounds, and I am satisfied that they can be made the finest in this country."[2]

Unfortunately, he and fair officials had very different ideas about the scheme for the grounds and the timeline. While the board wanted the new permanent fairgrounds to be developed in an intelligent, systematic fashion, they were insistent that it be ready for the Iowa State Fair in fifteen months. Shortly after being hired, however, Weidenmann, explained to the *Iowa State Register* that creating the fairgrounds "cannot be done in less than five years, and those who suppose that the work would all be completed for the fair of 1886, are of course very much mistaken." Given these disparate views, it was not surprising that shortly after Weidenmann submitted his plans in September 1885, the board decided to go in a different direction.[3]

After settling with Weidenmann, fair officials soon looked to up-and-coming Des Moines architect William Hackney. Hackney and his partner Mifflin Bell had acted as assistants to Alfred H. Piquenard, the architect of the Iowa State Capitol Building, and when he died in 1876, the two took over the project and oversaw its completion in 1886. In January 1886, ISAS leaders accepted Hackney's proposal "to make all plans, details, and specifications for buildings for the new Fairgrounds for 2½ percent of construction costs." After visiting other fairgrounds and considering the contours of the Thornton farm, Hackney laid out the Iowa State Fairgrounds. Then as now, the main entrance was located at East Thirtieth Street and Grand Avenue. Hackney intended to extend Grand Avenue from just inside the main entrance up a hill to the eastern side of the property, where the exhibition halls and campgrounds would be laid out. A 6,000-seat wooden amphitheater and half-mile racetrack complex would be located down the hill to the northwest. East of the track, agricultural equipment would be exhibited in the planned Power Hall and Machinery Row, and to the south, livestock barns and a dormitory for exhibitors would be erected.

Just to the south of the grounds where the Swine Barn sits today, the Chicago, Rock Island & Pacific Railroad (Rock Island) planned to build a passenger depot. When the fair began, the Rock Island expected to run passenger trains of ten coaches between downtown and the fairgrounds every seven to ten minutes.[4]

An army of 150 construction workers spent roughly three months turning Hackney's plans into reality. In a matter of months, they completed what architectural historian Thomas Leslie called "the single largest construction job in the state's history." Fifty-five buildings went up, and when added to the four that stood on the property when it was purchased and the eight that implement dealers and manufacturers constructed to showcase their equipment, sixty-seven major buildings graced the new permanent fairgrounds at the September opening of the 1886 Iowa State Fair.[5]

All the buildings were frame construction, generally clad in vertical board and batten siding, and required nearly a million board feet of lumber. Most impressive was the 10,000-square-foot Exposition Hall, which became the fair's signature structure. Modeled after London's famous Crystal Palace—the massive cast-iron and plate-glass pavilion built for the 1851 Great Exhibition—Exposition Hall's peaked roof and octagonal lantern tower added elements of grandeur. The building was flanked by smaller exhibition halls of similar design, all topped with shingled cupolas. One of these, originally known as Agricultural Hall, is today's Pioneer Hall.[6]

The *Iowa State Register* expressed delight at the progress of the fairgrounds and was one of the fair's biggest supporters. A week before the exhibition's new facility opened, the paper wrote: "The grounds and buildings are in excellent shape....It is believed to be one of the best State fairgrounds in the country. There is beautiful shape on the elevated land for protection from the heat of the sun, if the weather is clear and warm, and scores of large buildings for protection against inclement weather." The paper would continue in this cheerleading role, crowing about the fair and its importance and, when necessary, pushing for improvements to protect and promote the Iowa institution.[7]

Iowa State Agricultural Society officials had every reason to be proud of their new permanent home for the fair. Hackney's accomplishment was impressive; he had laid the grounds out in a practical and well-organized manner to ensure easy access to the barns and halls for livestock and machinery exhibitors, while placing the large amphitheater and track complex near the main entrance. He used the parcel's elevations to create impressive vistas from the exhibitions halls, which stood proudly overlooking the site. Regrettably, because neither Hackney's nor landscape architect Weidenmann's plans for the grounds exist, we do not know how much, if any, of the fairgrounds' design is attributable to Weidenmann. But we do know that although there were changes, the grounds were expanded, and a number of new buildings were erected over the next 130 years, the essential design of the fairgrounds with its distinct sections devoted to specific departments and activities remained largely intact.[8]

The new site saw record-setting attendance at the 1886 Iowa State Fair, and officials projected nothing but growth and prosperity for its future. But the next decade and a half proved exceedingly difficult and ended with a major change for the fair in 1900.

Several events, all beyond the control of the ISAS, rocked the Iowa State Fair and the apparent solid foundation the society had built. First was Seni-Om-Sed, a festival and parade the Des Moines Commercial Exchange—the forerunner of the Greater Des Moines Partnership—initially cooked up to boost fair attendance. Modeled after Mardi Gras in New Orleans, the event honored a mythical king of the harvest named "Seni-Om-Sed" (which was Des Moines spelled backward). With its exotic themes and boisterous parade, the first Seni-Om-Sed in 1889 drew a lot of attention and the praise of the ISAS. Fair secretary John Shaffer gushed about the Des Moines celebration, "In addition to the contribution of fifty thousand dollars toward securing a permanent home of the annual fairs; in addition to the liberal patronage bestowed in attendance and furnishing a thousand attractive and useful articles to the fair; in addition to the unpaid but cordially appreciated labor of its people in beautifying, ornamenting, and building upon the grounds... the capital city yet did more in organizing other features [Seni-Om-Sed] which were the incentive to bring thousands of strangers to enjoy the gala week, and to minister to their greater delight."[9]

Seni-Om-Sed grew even bigger the following year, with the parade alone attracting eighty-five thousand spectators, but the festivities and carnival soon became events solely designed to promote the capital city and its industry. Instead of drawing people to the fair, Seni-Om-Sed competed with the annual exhibition, and by 1894 a report on the fair stated, "The carnival and parade distracted urban patrons and contributed to declining revenues at the fair through the early 1890s."[10]

The fair faced other problems as well. The economy had fallen into deep depression in early 1893. Unemployment rose to 10 percent nationally and remained there for five years, violent labor strikes shook the country, and the emergent Populist movement grew. In Iowa and the Midwest, farmers were caught in a bind of high mortgage debt—taken on in prosperous times to buy more land and new equipment—coupled with plunging crop and livestock prices, making loan payments difficult. Bad weather and drought only worsened the situation, resulting in an ever increasing number of foreclosures and tax sales. The economy showed signs of a turnaround midway through the following year, but it dipped back into recession and did not recover until the summer of 1897.[11]

This troubled economy took its toll on fair attendance, which also faced stiff competition from the 1893 Columbian Exposition in Chicago. Dubbed the "White City" because of its stunning white buildings in neoclassical architecture set amid beautiful landscaped grounds, fountains, and a lake, the exposition also featured an exciting Midway filled with the latest in outdoor entertainments. It drew millions of visitors during its May through October run. The Iowa State Fair secretary tried to lessen the impact of this World's Fair by working with that year's production of Seni-Om-Sed. The Des Moines festival hired the Pain Pyrotechnic Company of Chicago to stage its spectacular fireworks show, "The Last Days of Pompeii," a reenactment of the eruption of Mount Vesuvius and the destruction of Pompeii. The ISAS board contributed $1,000 toward the program, hoping those who came for the show would go to the fair as well. The show ran ten days and was a huge success for Des Moines but fizzled for the agricultural society, for although visitors came to see the fireworks, they did not also patronize the fair.[12]

The 1893 fair left the ISAS with a $25,000 debt, and fair secretary John Shaffer resigned. He was followed by P. L. Fowler, who was able to get a $20,000 appropriation from state legislators because they proclaimed that the "fairs are of inestimable benefit to the state." The funding was a big help, but the society remained in the red. To restore the fair and right its finances, the new secretary focused on entertainment. The strategy put Fowler in step with county and state fair managers around the country who were moving in any way possible to emulate the attractions and entertainments that made the Columbian Exposition so successful. "My idea," he observed in 1895, "is to have something going on all the time and have so much that they [the patrons] cannot see it in one day and will have to come back." Thus, more sideshows, games, and rides were permitted in the fair's Midway, just south of the amphitheater on the western portion of the grounds.[13]

Likewise, the Fowler-led Iowa State Fairs offered a variety of bigger acts and performances, including balloon ascensions, high-wire aerial stunts, acrobats, daredevils—shot from cannons and parachuting to the ground or hurtling themselves from tall platforms into barrels of water—bicycle races, and a sensational collision of two railroad locomotives witnessed by an estimated crowd of fifty thousand to sixty thousand people. In 1896, Fowler even went so far as to paint the fair's buildings white and referred to it as Iowa's White City. But the effort fell short, as no one mistook the fair's repainted wood-frame structures for the neoclassical Beaux-Arts buildings of the Columbian Exposition, and the fair lost money again.[14]

These difficult years also ended any serious effort to implement the 1890 fairgrounds' master plan, which the board had had developed by landscape architect A. N. Carpenter. Carpenter's scheme included, for example, extensive landscaping, which had been generally left out of the original construction of the grounds in 1886, removal of some poorly located buildings, and setting aside land for future use. Although a number of smaller buildings had been added to keep up with growth, few serious changes took place on the fairgrounds. Electric lights and a power plant were added in 1891, and the amphitheater, badly damaged by a windstorm the following year, was replaced by two new structures.[15]

The fair of 1897 closed with $49 in the bank; the first time it had been in the black in five years, but its struggles continued. The following year, Omaha hosted a world's fair, the Trans-Mississippi and International Exposition, and because the ISAS board was still smarting from the Chicago Exposition, it avoided any rivalry with the Nebraska exhibition by cancelling its 1898 fair. The grounds ended up being used by the military that spring and summer during America's war with Spain.[16]

Although the fair was profitable the last year of the century, the trouble it experienced over the previous decade suggested the annual exhibition was too much for the private ISAS to handle. As historian Chris Rasmussen explained, "The agricultural society simply could not host a successful fair, maintain and improve the fairgrounds, and pay its expenses solely from gate receipts." Over the years, society officials had suggested their organization be placed under the auspices of state government and be involved more generally in economic development issues. After the 1899 fair, the society lobbied the legislature to eliminate the ISAS and replace it with a state entity.[17]

The Iowa General Assembly saw real value in the Iowa State Fair and was unwilling to see it fail. Legislators therefore acted accordingly, and in March 1900, they dissolved the ISAS and created the Iowa Department of Agriculture. The new agency assumed all the society's duties and was overseen by the Iowa State Board of Agriculture, which was entrusted with running the fair. Two decades later, in 1923, responsibility for managing the fair passed to the newly created Iowa State Fair Board.[18]

While the fair's move to Des Moines and the subsequent development of permanent fairgrounds had set it on the right path, putting the Iowa State Fair under the state's umbrella led to its renaissance. Over the next thirty years, the fairgrounds became a true Iowa landmark, something that Iowans in the late twentieth century decided was worth saving.

It was the state's good fortune to take over the fair just as better times returned. After experiencing record attendance in 1900, the fair enjoyed another big year in 1901. Now fair managers had several thousand dollars in the bank and could look to restore and update the fairgrounds. At that point, the booster *Iowa State Register* proclaimed it time to "Improve the State Fair." The paper called for cutting down on the dirt and mud on the grounds by paving roads and adding cement sidewalks. Even more critical, it agreed with former ISAS secretary P. L. Fowler's belief that "the state should erect exhibition halls [on the fairgrounds] worthy of the name, building them of brick and steel." These permanent structures would be far superior to the current exhibition halls, which were "nothing but large barns."[19]

Interest in improving the fair grew as the economy boomed; except for downturns following the Panic of 1907 and, later, the post–World War I recession, prosperity marked the first couple of decades of the twentieth century. This prosperity led city and state governments to consider building or rebuilding public structures. New thinking about urban planning and design had been sparked by Chicago's 1893 Columbian Exposition, with its White City and graceful grounds. There, Beaux-Arts neoclassical buildings and elegant surroundings had stressed order and beauty, and proponents argued that such architecture and landscaping could create moral and civic virtue among the populace. Daniel Burnham, one of the nation's foremost architects and urban designers, played a major role in developing the White City and became a leading advocate of these concepts, which coalesced in the City Beautiful Movement.[20]

Ideas from the movement took root in Des Moines's riverfront redevelopment, which eventually grew into the city's elegant seven-building Civic Center district. The project began piecemeal in 1899 with the construction of the three-story neoclassical Des Moines Public Library (now the headquarters for the World Food Prize). This was followed by a post office (now a county building), the Des Moines Coliseum (an arena that burned down in 1949), city hall, and the municipal courts building (now the police station). Elegant landscaping, fountains, new bridges, and a river walk ran throughout the district, which was later completed with the additions of the US Courthouse and the armory (now a city hall annex).[21]

After the 1901 fair, the Iowa State Board of Agriculture and its new secretary, John C. Simpson, thought "the time had arrived when the state should make appropriations for permanent improvement at the fairgrounds." The board agreed the most pressing need was a livestock pavilion, which they hoped would be the first in a number of new permanent brick facilities that would add grandeur and sophistication to the grounds. Clearly, board members had the City Beautiful Movement in mind as they considered these improvements for the fair. After getting the needed appropriation from the legislature, they retained Reeves and Baillie, a Peoria, Illinois, architectural firm, to design the brick and steel structure. The board situated the building near the center of the fairgrounds on the east side of Rock Island Avenue—the main north–south concourse through the fairgrounds that ran from the Rock Island depot to Grand Avenue—which was being paved with brick and concrete.[22]

The steel-framed oval pavilion went up in four months. A series of graceful arch-framed openings surrounded the building's exterior, which was clad in dark red brick and light stone trim. It was topped by a huge three-tiered roof with clerestory windows that worked in conjunction with the building's arches to provide ventilation. Inside, the stately structure boasted an immense arena that could seat up to two thousand spectators. The *Des Moines Register and Leader*, the successor paper to the *Iowa State Register*, applauded the new pavilion as "an artistic structure" that "would do credit to any city in the United States."[23]

Together, the new building and paving at the fairgrounds, coupled with good programming—including a return of the fireworks spectacular "The Last Days of Pompeii," this time held at the fairgrounds and not part of Seni-Om-Sed—made the 1902 fair "the greatest the state has ever seen," with receipts totaling a record $63,000. But it was more than that. The *Register and Leader* saw this exposition as the dawn of a new epoch at the fair, proclaiming in an August headline, "Exhibition This Year Marks Beginning of Something New and Modern."[24]

Indeed it did. The Livestock Pavilion was the first significant masonry and steel structure on the grounds. Besides employing new construction materials and techniques, the building's "vast scale and formal composition lent a new sense of dignity and importance to the events [held there]." Construction of the pavilion opened a major building program at the fairgrounds. Fair officials, aided by legislators interested in improving the fair and willing to appropriate funds to do so, erected a dozen major buildings over the next thirty years. The structures added an air of distinction and splendor to the grounds, and according to the fair officials' application to place the facility on the National Register of Historic Places in 1987, "formed the backbone of the present Fairgrounds."[25]

The next "permanent" building was intended for the exhibition of products from the agricultural, dairy, and horticultural departments. In early 1904, the board invited seven architectural firms—Reeves and Baillie of Illinois and six from Iowa—to submit plans for "a good,

substantial plain building...not too plain, but without costly decorations"
to be constructed with "stone, brick, iron, and wood."[26]

Smith & Gage of Des Moines won the job, possibly because architect
Oliver Smith, who drew the Beaux-Arts-inspired plans, had also designed
the impressive Iowa State Historical Building (now the Ola Babcock
Miller Building) as well as the new riverfront Des Moines Public Library
in that same style. The selection was significant for a couple of reasons.
First, Smith opted to use the same dark red brick and stone trim employed
earlier in the Livestock Pavilion. These materials and colors would
become a unifying theme throughout the grounds. Second, by hiring
Smith & Gage, the board had returned the fair to its architectural roots, for
the firm was a direct descendant of Bell & Hackney, which had designed
the original facilities. But more important, it began a longstanding
collaboration between the fair and architect Oliver Smith. He would be
associated with several Des Moines firms while doing work at the fair, but
shortly before he died, he partnered with Karl Keffer. This firm, initially
renamed Keffer & Jones, would continue the special relationship Smith
established with the fair, and its successor, Keffer/Overton, remains closely
involved with the institution today.[27]

Smith's new structure, named the Agriculture Building, was
constructed in 1904 north of the Livestock Pavilion. Much like exhibit
halls in the White City and the Iowa State Historical Building in Des
Moines, its majestic and imposing design suggested importance and
engendered civic pride in the fair. With domed entryways and barrel
dormers, the Agriculture Building joined the new Livestock Pavilion in
developing the modern fairground, which was rapidly taking shape.[28]

Livestock barns followed, all designed by firms where Oliver Smith
served as a principal, all clad in dark brick and light stone, and all
situated along the southern stretch of Rock Island Avenue, where the
barns had always been located. The Horse Barn and Swine Barn and
Pavilion initially went up in 1907, with additions and expansions soon
taking place on both, while the Cattle Barn and Sheep Barn, begun
in 1909 and 1915 respectively, were built in phases as well. Perhaps
the most visually interesting was the Sheep Barn, with terra-cotta ram
heads adorning the building's perimeter and blue-and-cream-colored
polychrome terra-cotta trim panels surrounding its entrances.[29]

While the barns were being erected, more activity ensued. Major structures were built that forever changed the fair's western section of Grand Avenue; the Fair Board retained one of the nation's leading landscape architects to develop a new master plan for the fairgrounds; and another important building went up east of the Agriculture Building.

In 1908 fair officials consolidated their various offices around the grounds in the large two-story, redbrick-and-stone-trimmed Administration Building, with a wide wrap-around porch on the first floor and a second-floor porch overlooking Grand Avenue. The new building was designed by the firm of Smith, Wetherell & Gage and immediately became one of the most popular at the fair. C. E. Cameron, president of the state board of agriculture, noted, "Of all the buildings that have been erected upon the Iowa State Fair Grounds in the last few years, none have called out so many favorable comments as the new Administration Building built this year. It not only throws all the offices of the fair together, so anyone wishing to go from one department to another can do so without traveling all over the grounds, but the building with its large rotunda and commodious porches was a mecca for all people attending the fair."[30]

When this most popular of structures was finished, officials had spent $358,000 on major improvements at the fair since 1902, funded by $199,000 from fair receipts and $148,000 from legislative appropriations. They had made great strides forward, but they worried that the building was not keeping pace with growing crowds and about the continuing deterioration of some current facilities, as well as enhancements being made at rival state fairs. That year the secretary listed ten needed projects; topping the list was "an amphitheater of fire proof construction, with a capacity of not less than 15,000."[31]

The wooden grandstands, hastily built after a storm destroyed the original in 1892, had been a concern for several years. They were now too small for some of the larger events and shows, and timbers were rotting. In 1907, the board of agriculture asked architect Oliver Smith to draw plans for a new amphitheater and swine barn and then asked the legislature for $150,000 for the two structures. When it became clear that only half the request would be funded, hog producers lobbied hard for the new barn, and the amphitheater was put on hold.[32]

But the Fair Board members did not have to wait long. Two years later, the general assembly appropriated $100,000 for a new grandstand and track, located slightly west of the original facility. Planned as a two-phased project, the first portion consisted of a gently curved, unadorned steel and concrete open stadium structure with a wide roof that seated ten thousand and was situated at the finish line of the half-mile track. But phase two was delayed for eighteen years. In 1927, additions increased the Grandstand's seating by five thousand, while its exterior was finally enclosed with a formal facing of redbrick and stone trim, while neoclassical arches topped with windows ran along the entire south face of the structure, making it, according to preservation architect William Wagner, "almost Coliseum in feeling." The ornamental façade tied the Grandstand to the other Beaux-Arts buildings already adorning the fairgrounds, and with military-themed decorations that included two American eagles in relief, it was dedicated to the soldiers lost in the First World War. Beneath the stadium seats, exhibit areas, classrooms, and a small auditorium were installed. When completed, the truly monumental building was six hundred feet long, the largest in Iowa at the time.[33]

Well before the second phase of the Grandstand's construction took place, the Fair Board moved to ensure that the future development proceeded in an orderly fashion and commissioned another comprehensive plan for the fairgrounds. In 1910 it invited several prominent landscape architects to submit bids for the task. One, Frederick Law Olmstead Jr., who with his brother had continued his famous father's landscape practice, turned down the offer because his schedule was full. Ultimately, O. C. Simonds of Chicago, another well-known figure in the profession and a founder of the American Society of Landscape Architects, was selected to create a new master plan. Trained as a civil engineer and architect, Simonds moved into landscape design with his work on Chicago's Graceland Cemetery, using native plantings to transform it into a vast pastoral parklike setting. From there, he moved on to lay out other cemeteries, parks, golf courses, college campuses—he provided plans for the Iowa State College of Agricultural and Mechanical Arts (now Iowa State University) in 1902–03—and private estates, including the Brucemore mansion and grounds in Cedar Rapids.[34]

Simonds's master plan started with the current fairgrounds, and although he proposed many new buildings, landscaping, and roads, he confirmed the soundness of the original configuration and land use at the facility. Most of his ideas did not come to fruition, but those that did included his recommendation to move the Midway to a permanent location just east of the Grandstand and racetrack, his proposal to organize and plat the campground, and perhaps most important to the Fair Board, his call for the erection of a new machinery exhibit hall on Grand Avenue, just west of the Administration Building.[35]

This last project had been on the Fair Board's wish list for several years. The board had long wanted to add a new structure with some of the unifying architectural features of recent permanent buildings for exhibiting the latest in machinery and implements. The proposal gained traction in early 1911, when the legislature appropriated $65,000 for the hall. Not surprisingly, the board again turned to architect Smith, who at the time had partnered with another group, Smith, Liebbe, Nourse, and Rasmussen, to design the building. As construction began, the Fair Board condemned and tore down the ragtag assortment of twelve private exhibition halls manufacturers and dealers such as John Deere, Global Machinery and Supply, and Ohio Cultivator had erected to display their latest equipment along old Machinery Row just east of the Grandstand. Here, on Simonds's suggestion, they relocated the Midway.[36]

A brick and steel structure, Machinery Hall (renamed the Varied Industries Building in 1936) was built over two years; it was opened for the 1911 fair and completed the following year. The 100,000-square-foot open-air pavilion had a low brick wall and was covered by a wide roof supported by a metal truss system, making it one of the largest such facilities in the Midwest. Over the entryways on the northeast and northwest corners, Smith employed neoclassical touches such as half-barrel roofs, which he had used earlier in the Agriculture Building and Swine Barn. The hall's grand entryway, in the words of architect William Wagner, consisted of "wide piers on either side of the main entrance...surmounted by a frieze and a pediment. The side piers carry up and are capped with a decorative pagoda and flag pole."[37]

Oliver Smith went on to design one more primary structure at the fairgrounds—the Women's and Children's Building—before he died in 1916. Years earlier, in 1903, fair secretary Simpson had tried making the grounds more attractive to women by converting the old Horticulture Hall into a women's building, intended as a place where women and children could catch their breath and rest amid the hubbub of the fair. Nearly a decade later, women's groups pushed fair officials for a building dedicated to women's activities. The general assembly provided funds for such a structure in 1913, and Smith was commissioned for the job.[38]

Dedicated at the 1914 fair, the new structure was located at the end of a landscaped walkway heading east up the hill between the Agriculture Building and the Livestock Pavilion. The two-story u-shaped structure was clad in red brick, trimmed in white stone, and had a red tile roof. Its broad porch provided a spot to sit with a pleasant view of the fairgrounds. In addition to exhibit space, a fireproof art gallery, a nursery, a playroom, and a dining room, the building featured a 700-seat auditorium, where programs devoted to homemaking, nutrition, and childrearing were held. In its comments on the 1914 Iowa State Fair, the *Breeder's Gazette* observed that the new Women's and Children's Building marked "a distinct and significant departure in fair grounds equipment. Iowa says thereby to the world that the care of infants and the education of the mothers are of as much importance to the state as the improvement of pigs and other farm stock. It is time that such a note was sounded."[39]

Two final buildings of consequence were erected on the fairgrounds during the 1920s. One grew out of the Fair Board's understanding that amusements were an important component of the exhibition, while the other arose from the fair's educational mission. First to go up was the Ye Old Mill, the oldest permanent amusement ride on the fairgrounds. Such rides had been around since the turn of the century. The Iowa State Fair's was built by John Keenan, a Philadelphia owner of vaudeville theaters and an early developer of such attractions. His mill rides gently floated patrons in two-passenger boats through dark, enclosed canals, which allowed a few moments of privacy and romance for couples. The churning of a waterwheel located on the outside of the "mill building" generated a current that propelled the boats through the water, thus resulting in the ride's name. The first versions of his Ye Old Mill were installed in Little Rock, Arkansas, and Oklahoma City, Oklahoma. By 1915, the Minnesota State Fair had a Ye Old Mill, and the Iowa State Fair Board was discussing adding one.[40]

That year, the Fair Board contacted Keenan-Mahan Construction Company to build and operate a roller coaster on the fairgrounds and considered a Ye Old Mill attraction as well. Nothing came of the latter idea until 1920, when the board moved ahead, hiring Keenan-Mahan to erect, own, and operate the Ye Old Mill for a percentage of the ticket receipts. The 1,500-foot-long canal ride was located on Grand Avenue, just east of the entrance to the Midway. It opened for the 1920 fair.[41]

Meanwhile, an educational attraction west of the Grandstand was being contemplated as well. Since 1910, the Iowa Department of Fish and Game (now incorporated into the Iowa Department of Natural Resources) had held exhibits at the fairgrounds to familiarize Iowans with its work. It offered programs and presentations under the cover of tents, as well as native game animals and steel cattle tanks stocked with fish from Iowa's streams, rivers, and lakes. In 1920, William Albert, a longtime deputy warden in the department, was named warden. An advocate of these educational outreach efforts at the Iowa State Fair, Albert thought they should be housed in a permanent, dignified structure. His efforts to obtain such a building finally paid off when, six years later, the Department of Fish and Game commissioned architects Proudfoot, Rawson & Souers to design it.[42]

In 1926, the aquarium was built, replacing the stock tanks and offering a much better view of the aquatic life. Then, over the next three years, a redbrick pavilion went up around the aquarium, finally topped by a roof in 1929. According to architectural historians David Gebhard and Gerald Mansheim, the structure represented "a 1920s version of a small mid-fifteenth century Italian Renaissance building. A three-arched loggia projects toward the street [Grand Avenue] and to each side are high double-arched windows with metal balconies." Also of note, they explained, were the "wonderful sculpted swans poised on the corners of the roof." Unlike the other major "permanent" structures that had been erected and were built and owned by the Fair Board, this new pavilion had been constructed and paid for by the Iowa Department of Fish and Game.[43]

Its completion marked the end of the massive building program begun by the Fair Board in 1902, reinforcing the fairgrounds' original layout and adorning it with graceful, stately facilities. By the end of the 1920s, the exhibition's future had been cast literally in stone and brick. If attendance numbers were any indication, the Fair Board's decisions and a cooperative legislature had put the Iowa State Fair in good stead. In 1904, the year the Agriculture Building had gone up, and two years after the Livestock Pavilion was completed, fair attendance stood at 125,000. The figure more than doubled in seven years, and in 1929 it would peak at 435,000, an impressive three times larger than the entire population of Des Moines. To paraphrase that magical quotation from *Field of Dreams*, the 1989 hit film set in Iowa, "If you built it, they will come." The Fair Board had rightly banked on the idea that a well-planned fairground with imposing, impressive buildings would generate civic pride and expand the institution. Certainly the fair's many programs themselves, the exhibits, displays, contests, attractions, entertainment, and Midway rides, played a critical role in the rising numbers as well, but the beautiful grounds and facilities lured fairgoers in and kept them coming back.[44]

Nothing, however, could avert the adverse impact of the Great Depression. Fair attendance plummeted, and the exhibition struggled through the decade. But that same year, during the depths of the economic downturn, the fair received unexpected publicity when Iowa native Phil Stong published his novel, *State Fair*. The book recounted the story of the Frake family, who made their annual trek from their southeastern Iowa farm outside the fictional town of Brunswick to Des Moines and the Iowa State Fair. Abel Frake hoped to win the best-in-show award for his prize hog, Blue Boy; his wife, Melissa, sought blue ribbons for her mincemeat pie and pickles, and their teenage children pursued fun and romance.[45]

Although Stong had penned a novel, he knew Iowa and the fair. He was born and raised in a small town in southeastern Iowa, his grandfather had served as swine superintendent at the Iowa State Fair, and in the early 1920s as a reporter for the *Des Moines Register*, Stong covered livestock shows at the fair. When *State Fair* came out in the spring of 1932, it was an immediate success. Stong soon signed a movie deal, and Fox Studio crews were at the fair that summer taking atmospheric and background shots for the film.[46]

The movie opened the following year and starred Will Rogers, Janet Gaynor, and Lew Ayres. It was a box office sensation and was nominated for an Academy Award for best picture. The book and this initial film—there would be two more versions, the Rodgers and Hammerstein musical adaption in 1945 and the 1962 remake with new songs by Richard Rodgers, as well as a 1996 Broadway musical—showcased the fair, although the story had a sentimental tinge and largely avoided the harsh economic realities and growing urban–rural divide of the period. Stong's story portrayed content Midwestern farmers who, in the words of historian Chris Rasmussen, were "cheerful, prosperous, and utterly content with farm life." But most important for the Fair Board and the people of Des Moines and Iowa, the upbeat tale introduced millions of Americans to the Iowa State Fair, making the exhibition an iconic representation of what state fairs were or should be.[47]

The hoopla and attention generated by the book and film acted as a coming out party for the fair, a symbolic pat on the back for the Fair Board and its decades of planning and hard work. But in the mid-1930s, one had to wonder if the fair's best days were already behind it. And when the economy did recover, would future generations of fair managers and legislators have the savvy and political will to address cultural changes, keeping the fair vibrant and relevant?

THE COMING OF
THE BLUE RIBBON FOUNDATION

When the Iowa State Fair Livestock Pavilion opened in 1902, the *Des Moines Register and Leader* (now the *Des Moines Register*) noted a seismic shift at the fairgrounds, declaring that "A Twentieth Century State Fair" had commenced. It applauded fair leadership for reimagining the fairgrounds and initiating the period of building that resulted in the imposing redbrick and stone structures that would soon grace the site. Years later, however, the headline seemed satiric. This "modern" fairground was completed by 1929, but few updates took place over the next sixty-odd years. By 1991, *Des Moines Register* editorial writer Rox Laird lamented that "succeeding generations of fair managers have patched and repaired as best they could," but the core of the fairgrounds remained largely unchanged, hosting the fair in its ever-aging facilities through the close of the twentieth century.[1]

From the Great Depression and World War II through the vastly different postwar world, the Iowa State Fair Board endeavored to keep the exhibition relevant and continue drawing crowds amid the many changes. Of course, there were some additions to the fairgrounds, but few were significant, and fair officials largely made do with routine maintenance on increasingly outmoded and overcrowded buildings. Serious concerns about the fairgrounds' deteriorating conditions were finally raised in the 1960s, beginning what became a thirty-year period of fair officials seeking solutions and funding to restore the grounds. Committees were formed, consultants were hired, and plans were developed. Some were implemented, but none worked. With few options remaining, the fair manager and Fair Board settled on the untested idea of developing a fund-raising organization, which became known as the Iowa State Fair Blue Ribbon Foundation.

Decades before the foundation was created, the fair was struggling through the tough years of the Great Depression. Attendance tumbled from a record high of 435,000 in 1929 to 256,000 in 1932, its lowest point in seventeen years. From there it gradually recovered, getting a special boost in 1938 when the Iowa Territorial Centennial Commission, which oversaw a celebration marking the one hundredth anniversary of the creation of the Iowa Territory, chose that year's fair as the concluding event to the statewide festivities. Special exhibits throughout the fair depicted the past century of Iowa's history. Attendance jumped to 430,000, an increase of nearly 15 percent over the previous year. Although the crowd thinned out somewhat in 1939, it appeared that the fair's good times had returned.[2]

At the same time, two new facilities rose on the fairgrounds. In 1938 the Public Works Administration (PWA), a New Deal work relief agency, and the Iowa State Legislature together funded the new Poultry Building (now the Bruce L. Rastetter 4-H Exhibits Building), directly west of the Sheep Barn. Much more important, however, was the 4-H Club Building (now the Oman Family Youth Inn), the first significant structure to be built in a decade. This was a joint venture of the legislature and the Works Progress Administration (WPA), another New Deal work relief agency. It was designed by longtime fair architects Keffer and Jones and went up from 1939 to 1942. Art deco in design, the poured concrete structure had rounded corners with glass block and dramatically broke with the fair's theme of red brick and classical architecture. It was situated east of the Swine Barn and housed a dormitory, dining hall, and an auditorium for boys exhibiting animals at the fairgrounds.[3]

Just as the fair was gaining momentum, international events intervened. Several months after the United States entered World War II in December 1941, the US Army Air Corps asked for permission to store equipment and supplies in the fairground's major buildings for the duration of the war. The board agreed but still hoped to hold a smaller exhibition until the federal government requested that all major fairs be cancelled in an effort to conserve tires and gasoline. The board complied, suspending the fair until the war was over. This was only the second time that the fair had been cancelled; the first had occurred forty-four years earlier because of the World's Fair in Omaha and the Spanish-American War.[4]

The fair reopened four years later in 1946, and as the board had done eight years earlier, it again stressed state history by celebrating the centennial of Iowa statehood. War weary Iowans were ready for the fair's return and poured through the gates. Attendance soared to 514,000, topping the half-million mark for the first time. But attendance would fall back from this high point over the next years except for a temporary bump in 1951, when the fair's run was expanded from eight to ten days. The centennial fair in 1954 emphasized nostalgia once more, going so far as to construct a full-size model of the first Iowa State Fair in Fairfield on the north side of the grounds. Here events from the first fair were reenacted. Iowans responded in large numbers again, and fair attendance set a new record of 607,000.[5]

Shortly after the fair's postwar reopening, another significant addition went up on the grounds. Similar in design to the recently erected 4-H Club Building (Oman Family Youth Inn), the three-story poured concrete Girls' 4-H Dormitory (now the Patty and Jim Cownie Cultural Center) was also designed by Keffer and Jones and built in 1949. Unlike the other structure, which had been paid for with funds from the Iowa General Assembly and WPA, this new $417,000 facility was entirely paid for out of fair earnings.[6]

Unfortunately, the following year the fairgrounds lost an important original structure when Exposition Hall, which had adorned the fair's hilltop since 1886, succumbed to the ravages of time. With its lantern tower, the hall had long been "one of the show-spots of the grounds." But, the *Des Moines Tribune* continued, "it grew old and out of fashion." After the state fire marshal declared it a fire hazard, fair officials tore down the aging wood-frame building in 1950. Yet the demolition set off no alarm bells about deteriorating conditions at the grounds. Instead, its removal was seen as a sign of progress. According to architectural historian Thomas Leslie, "The fair board essentially trimmed the grounds' nostalgic image, eliminating the symbol of the previous century's difficult growth and leaving in place the brick barns, grandstand, and livestock pavilion as the fair's primary architectural icons...which maintained the fair's more progressive image." This left Pioneer Hall as the lone major building from the original construction on the grounds.[7]

But progress at the fair was not assured. The economic and social landscape that fair officials had successfully navigated before World War II had shifted, and the exhibition faced a very different postwar climate. An economic boom, along with rapid advances in science and technology, ushered in great change, and agriculture, still the basis for the fair, experienced a revolution. Farms got bigger as mechanization and economics of scale spread into the countryside, and small family farms declined. From 1945 to 1964, the average farm more than doubled in size, but the number of farms decreased more than 40 percent. As people left farming and headed for urban areas, many small towns that dotted the countryside slowly withered and died. The world the fair had highlighted seemed to be fading away.[8]

Meanwhile, urban expansion was led by rapid suburban growth that dominated the period. Here a new consumer culture took root, pushed by the baby boom. By 1960, most families had at least one automobile in the driveway, and nearly nine of ten American homes had a television, with the average viewer watching it more than five hours a day. Popular programs such as *Ozzie and Harriet* or *Father Knows Best* depicted the idealized family as white and middle class living in the suburbs, with the husband working a white-collar job and the wife staying at home and caring for the children.[9]

Set against this suburban-centric fast-paced society, where Iowans moved along new interstate highways and flew to destinations in jet airplanes, the Iowa State Fair appeared a quaint throwback to a bygone era. Fair attendance only reinforced this view, falling by nearly a third from its peak in 1954 by the end of the decade. How could the fair remain relevant and attractive? What adjustments could be made, or what could be added to appeal to an audience that was rapidly becoming more and more removed from agriculture? And what about the fairgrounds itself? Could it continue to accommodate the fair?

The Fair Board and fair secretary Lloyd Cunningham realized their most successful fairs following World War II had celebrated the state's past, and after the centennial fair in 1954, they sought to capitalize on this interest in Iowa history by building Heritage Village. Set along Grand Avenue east of the Ye Old Mill, the area featured old Iowa structures, either actual historic buildings moved from their original location to the fair or replicas built on-site. Ten years later, new fair manager Kenny Fulk made even better use of Heritage Village when he introduced the first of five heritage-themed fairs. Each emphasized a particular era of Iowa history, and each year saw a new addition to the village. The first focused on the Native American period in Iowa (up to 1800) and included the construction of two wickiups erected by Meskwaki Indians from Tama.[10]

Themed fairs proved a good way to market the fair, and after the historical fairs ended in 1969, they were succeeded by several focusing on the present, beginning in 1970 with "Discover Iowa." The use of themes continues today as a means to advertise and promote each annual fair.

Several years after Heritage Village was begun, the board made another move to appeal to a broader Iowa audience, when in 1959 it agreed with local radio personality Bill Riley's proposal that he host a talent search at the fair. Riley's ties to the annual summer exhibition dated back to 1946, when he began broadcasting a KRNT radio variety program from the fair. The new program, Bill Riley Talent Search, hosted qualifying contests at county fairs and exhibitions throughout the state with winners competing at the Iowa State Fair. It quickly became one of the most beloved traditions at the fair, and when Riley retired in 1996, the fair's Plaza Stage, where the talent search was held, was renamed the Bill Riley Stage. The show remains a fair staple today, with Bill Riley Jr. now overseeing and hosting the competition.[11]

Riley became involved in other aspects of the fair, and after 1962, he and fair manager Fulk began discussing ways to make it more appealing to urban and suburban young people. They came up with Teen Town, a pavilion and stage set on the western side of the grounds that opened in 1964. It featured live rock music, dancing, and a variety of exhibits and vendors catering to youth culture.[12]

More important was the revamping of Grandstand entertainment, which by the 1960s was losing $20,000 per year. Up to that point, acts at the Grandstand were generally variety-type shows. To draw larger crowds and put the fair in the mainstream, Fulk went after bigger name entertainers, beginning with Iowa native Andy Williams, who attracted a large audience over five nights in 1965. The fair grossed $20,000 from Williams's performances. This success was followed by a string of stars playing the Grandstand, including Red Skelton, Johnny Cash, and Bob

Hope. Over the next few years, pop groups and figures such as The Jackson Five, Sonny and Cher, Chicago, and Elton John played the venue and were immensely popular.[13]

All these efforts paid off, pushing attendance back over six hundred thousand by 1967. But as attendance continued to rise, Fulk noticed problems with the fairgrounds itself. Designed in the railroad era, the complex was not automobile friendly. Parking was inadequate and interstate access poor. Then there were the main buildings. With the exception of the Girls' 4-H Dormitory, all predated World War II, with most having been erected before World War I. The old structures were outdated, increasingly expensive to maintain, and inadequate for larger crowds. At the urging of Fulk and Fair Board members, the Iowa State Legislature created a committee in 1965 to consider long-term options for maintaining the fair as a major state event and increasing its significance over time.[14]

Made up of fair officials and government and educational leaders, the committee examined several options, including updating current facilities or relocating the fairgrounds to a new location—one suggestion put the new fairground west of Des Moines along Hickman Road and Interstates 80-35 near Living History Farms. Also under discussion was the possibility of hosting a World's Fair focused on agriculture and food on the same grounds. The one-time event would highlight Iowa's agrarian heritage, attract large numbers of people and tourist dollars, and help fund new fairgrounds or redevelop the current one. The committee eventually recommended that the Fair Board retain Economic Research Associates (ERA), a Los Angeles-based consulting firm with expertise in tourism and recreation economics. Its principals had, in fact, worked on an early feasibility study for Southern California's Disneyland in the mid-1950s and then came together to form ERA. Since then, they had done planning research for a number of major exhibitions, including the Montreal Expo, the Texas State Fair, the Wisconsin State Fair, and San Antonio's HemisFair.[15]

Completed in 1968, ERA's report examined the alternatives of modernizing the present fairgrounds with or without hosting a world food expo or building new fairgrounds with or without holding the expo. The consultants suggested two options: either the less expensive, less risky updating of the current fairgrounds without the world food expo or the much costlier but potentially more rewarding alternative of building a new fairground with the expo staged there. Costs varied widely; updating the current complex was estimated at $6.3 million, while new facilities were projected to require $58.5 million. If estimated operating revenues for the world food expo as well as those of the Iowa State Fair at the new complex were considered, the cost of new fairgrounds fell to a more manageable $10.3 million, but this remained almost twice as high as refurbishing the current facility.[16]

Based on its own work and the ERA study, the committee recommended that the Fair Board pursue the new fairgrounds, where the world food expo would also be held. It was clear, however, that the funding for this big-ticket project was not there, and in an ironic twist, this lack of money saved the historic fairgrounds. The status quo prevailed, and the fair stayed put, but the once grand buildings grew more outdated and dilapidated. Don Greiman, who served on the Fair Board for over forty years, remembered that by the 1970s, "Our facilities were getting so run down that exhibitors would get upset, and I couldn't blame them. We just had to say to them, 'We appreciate your putting up with it, but this is the situation we're in and we're doing our best.'"[17]

Fulk continued seeking creative ways to fund the fair, including the addition of pari-mutuel betting on horse racing, but nothing initially came of the idea. Meanwhile, the difficult economy of the mid-1970s cut into fair revenue, putting it in the red by 1976, and Fulk resigned as fair manager to run for Congress but was defeated by Democrat Tom Harkin.[18]

The board looked to Jim Taylor, then manager of the successful Heart of Illinois Fair, a regional exhibition in Peoria, to replace Fulk. Taylor's immediate focus was on "making payroll" and turning the fair around. While watching spending, he worked on expanding and improving free entertainment, an approach that had been successful in bringing people through the gate at his previous job in Illinois. Taylor brought in higher quality free acts, including the then popular "Dancing Waters" fountains, opened the Iowa State Fair Museum, and added a new free entertainment stage west of the Cultural Center (now remodeled and expanded as the MidAmerican Energy Stage). North of the stage, he and the board erected the Earth Home (now the offices of the Blue Ribbon

Foundation) as a key attraction for the 1983 fair. He also established the fair's initial public relations department, and for the first time, the fair began selling its own souvenirs, including caps, hats, and shirts.[19]

These moves helped boost attendance and restored the fair to profitability, but they did not address the longer-term issue of the deteriorating facilities. For this, Taylor and the board persuaded the legislature to create an Iowa State Fair master planning committee, charged with investigating options for the fair's future. Established in 1978, the committee retained two consultants, ERA, which was familiar with the fair because of its work a decade earlier, and POD Inc., a California-based landscape architectural firm, to study different options for the fair's future. Once again, a key issue was whether or not to remain at the current location.[20]

While the study was being conducted, the committee voted down the alternatives that called for developing new fairgrounds at another site because their costs, ranging from $35 million to $50 million, were much too expensive. The ERA/POD report was completed in spring 1979 and emphasized the significance of the historic structures on the grounds. It stressed the importance of preserving them as the major thrust of the redevelopment of the fairgrounds. Eric Lassen, a POD architect involved in the study, referred to these facilities as "a cherished part of Iowa history" and believed the fair might be in line for federal grants if it were listed on the National Register of Historic Places.[21]

Actually, at the behest of the Fair Board, staff had already begun the application process for placing particular fair structures on the federal historic register. But with the encouragement of this report and Iowa's nominations review committee, which suggested the entire fairground be included, Bill Fisher, assistant manager of the fair, changed course and began researching the whole site to list as an historic district. Fisher worked closely with Floyd Deets, longtime superintendent of the grounds, and William Wagner, a local preservation architect, to complete the research. In early 1987, the Fair Board hired William Page, a Des Moines public historian, who drafted the application and worked with Iowa's State Historic Preservation Office to submit it to the National Park Service, which oversees the National Register of Historic Places. The application was successful, and that September, the Iowa State Fair and Exposition Grounds were added to the historic register. Inclusion on this list did not lead to federal grants as the ERA/POD consultants believed, but it would prove helpful in raising money down the road.[22]

Although the study had emphasized preservation, it sadly identified the Women's and Children's Building and the Administration Building as too far gone for restoration and recommended demolition. The former was in much worse shape, requiring a new roof and significant work on the foundation. Repair costs were estimated at $700,000, well beyond the means of the Fair Board, and as suggested, it was torn down in 1980. The Administration Building remained in place, with short-term patching keeping it serviceable as it awaited major renovation.[23]

Armed with the consultants' work, the master planning committee presented its final report to the legislature in 1980. With a goal of making the fair economically self-sufficient, it called for a vast redevelopment of the fairgrounds. This included preserving and rehabilitating historic structures while at the same time modernizing the complex by adding new exhibit facilities, more parking, and improving the site's year-round capability. Although significantly less expensive than moving the fairgrounds, the plan required millions of dollars to implement. To finance the plan, the ERA/POD consultants picked up on an idea Fulk had floated earlier: since it looked like the Iowa State Legislature might open the state to horse racing and pari-mutuel betting, the fair should consider hosting racing on its grounds. This, along with state appropriations and possibly construction bonds, was seen as a means of financing the plan, which would cost approximately $23 million, or $32 million if new horse racing facilities were added.[24]

Estimates did suggest that horse racing could be lucrative for the fair. According to ERA official Raymond Braun, the fairgrounds could accommodate horse racing by enlarging the track and adding a clubhouse. The expansion would be well worth it, Braun believed, as he suggested a sixty-day racing season "could mean an income to the fair of over $1.6 million the first year and over $2 million by 1985."[25]

Support for pari-mutuel wagering grew in the legislature as the farm crisis hit the state in the early 1980s, and many saw it as a means to help the horse industry. It was legalized in 1983. Soon the newly created Iowa

Racing Commission (now the Iowa Racing and Gaming Commission) was issuing licenses for horse and dog racing. But a year before harness racing was sanctioned for the Iowa State Fair and several county fairs in 1985, plans for Prairie Meadows Race Track in Altoona, a northeastern suburb of Des Moines, were approved.[26]

The announcement dampened enthusiasm for horse racing at the fair, and plans for additions to the track were shelved. Still, betting machines were installed, and four much- abbreviated harness racing seasons were held at the fairgrounds from 1985 through 1988. The first year's races were held over four days in June and another four days in early August, but instead of making money, the fair's racing operation showed a loss. The racing season was extended to twenty days by 1987, and it moved into the black, but it never came close to providing the windfall officials had hoped.[27]

Even before horse racing at the fair had begun, the board was investigating other funding possibilities. In 1984 Taylor and the board invited Howard Braren and Ray German of Howard Braren Associates (now BMG Associates Inc.), a Davenport, Iowa-based fund-raising firm, to discuss how the fair might go about raising money. The company was hired later that year to do a feasibility study. Braren believed "it was crucial to have Des Moines leaders behind the project" and soon identified key players in the community. He and Taylor then met with these movers and shakers, including Bill Knapp, one of the state's foremost real estate developers, John Ruan, head of a Des Moines trucking and banking operation, Tom Urban, chairman of Pioneer Hi-Bred International (now DuPont Pioneer), the nation's largest seed company, and officials of Deere & Company, a leading manufacturer of agricultural machinery, about the fair's needs and a possible fund-raising campaign.[28]

Hindsight suggested that the Fair Board and Braren were on the right track. Money from the private sector would be critical to restoring the fairgrounds, while involving Des Moines leadership would also prove important. The particular individuals and firms Braren approached about funding the project were also right, as all mentioned above would play prominent roles in the site's restoration. But that was down the road, and in 1985 the timing was not right. The farm crisis was still a drag on the Iowa economy, making it a tough time for a fund-raising campaign. And the Des Moines community did not warm to the idea; leaders did not know much about the fair or express much interest in it. "They did not see it as theirs; it was still viewed as a farmers' fair," recalled Judy Nye, founder of the Iowa State Fair Singers.[29]

The fund-raising idea was shelved for the moment. Meanwhile, Jim Taylor decided that after restoring the fair's finances and developing a master plan for the grounds, it was time to move on, and in early 1986, he took a position at the American Royal Livestock Show in Kansas City. The board hired Marion Lucas, director of the Missouri State Fair, to replace him.[30]

Although the fair was now in a much better place than it had been a decade earlier, the grounds were not. Buildings continued deteriorating, and for some, the situation was becoming desperate. In 1987, the Iowa State Legislature asked Lucas and the board yet again for a study comparing the costs of restoring the fairgrounds versus moving and building a new complex. Staff, including Bill Hare, the fairground's plant operations manager, and Gary Slater, future manager of the fair, worked on the report, as did James Rowing, head of the construction engineering department at Iowa State University. Completed in 1988, the study came to the same conclusion of earlier reports: the cost of restoring the current fairgrounds was estimated at $29.4 million (or $32.4 when the 10 percent contingency fund was included), significantly less than the $142 million needed for a new facility.[31]

This report finally put to rest any discussion of moving the fair, and with legislative support, the board prepared a ten-year, $30 million fund-raising campaign to renovate the fairgrounds. Interestingly, much like at the turn of the century, when both Des Moines and the Iowa State Fair forged ahead with a massive building program sparked by the City Beautiful Movement, the fair's plans to rehabilitate its aging facilities coincided with a renaissance already underway in the city's long-neglected downtown core.

In light of consultant Howard Braren's finding that major financial support from Des Moines leaders would not be forthcoming, partially, at least, because of their focus on rebuilding downtown, the board prepared a three-phase approach seeking the money from other sources. First was

Fan Fair. The "brainchild" of Bill Riley, Fan Fair was first offered at the 1988 fair. For a $25 annual donation, Fan Fair members received two tickets to the following year's fair and an opportunity to buy two Grandstand show tickets before they were offered to the general public. The program increased awareness of the fair's needs and did bring in some money—months after it was announced, Fan Fair had raised $25,000—but the amount did not make much of a dent in the millions required. Still, Fan Fair remained in place and continues to generate money for the fair today.[32]

For the major chunk of renovation funds, the board initiated phase two of the campaign, which sought annual appropriations from the Iowa General Assembly of $2.5 million for each of the next ten years. As always, the board had continued using fair revenue to maintain the fairground—from 1985 through 1987, for example, it spent $1.35 million on building repairs—but as Marion Lucas explained in 1988, "Our needs are so critical, the deterioration so extensive, we cannot do what must be done without massive help from the Legislature." To assist in this ambitious undertaking, the board hired legislative lobbyist Gene Kennedy, but their efforts fell short. In 1989 and 1990, the board's requests for $5 million in state assistance yielded only $1.3 million, not nearly enough to cover the fair's most critical needs, then identified as $2.6 million required for Grandstand repairs, $680,000 for work on the Varied Industries Building, $700,000 for a new roof on the Sheep Barn, and $680,000 for sidewalks.[33]

The situation grew worse, with Lucas reporting, "We have been told not to expect any State funding for the next three years [1991–1993], but the intensifying deterioration of our facilities compels us to act. We must find new sources of income."[34]

Even with the addition of the third component of the fund-raising drive—higher fees at the fair—the campaign fell far short of its large goals. In 1990, the board and Lucas began investigating a new option: creating a separate foundation, possibly headed by a professional fund-raiser, to find the millions needed for restoring the fairground. Such a move put Iowa State Fair officials in largely unchartered waters. Although the Nebraska State Fair had established such a foundation in 1989, it was brand new and did not have a proven track record, so as board member Paul Vaassen recalled, "We relied on information from corporations that had foundations, or individuals that had foundations, and worked from there."[35]

The real work began the following January, when board president Dave Huinker appointed a fund-raising committee of board members Paul Vaassen, who served as chair, Mel Shanda, Bobbie Finch— Governor Terry Branstad's legislative liaison—and Jan Higgins, the assistant manager of the fair. Huinker sat in on the committee as well.[36]

After a consultant suggested that a fund-raising campaign could be successful and a foundation was the right way to go about it, the board approved the idea in principle, and the subcommittee laid the groundwork by studying a variety of foundations. Higgins and Finch worked with the Iowa Attorney General's office and the Brown, Winick, Graves, Donnelly, Baskerville and Schoenebaum law firm to obtain tax exempt 501(c)(3) status for the new organization, making any contributions to it tax deductible.[37]

In the midst of these efforts, *Des Moines Register* editorial writer Rox Laird penned a op-ed essay in August 1991 calling the Iowa State Fairgrounds "a disgrace" and implored Iowans to "dedicate themselves to restoring [the] former luster to this treasure." Although Laird was not in close touch with fair officials, he had heard murmurs of the direction in which the board was moving. He knew that up to $32 million were needed for fairground repairs and believed "a major capital-improvement program is in order, financed through a combination of state and private money." Then, with a sentence that the state fair public relations department could not have written any better, Laird declared, "Instead of allowing the Iowa State Fairgrounds to become a curious relic from an earlier century, Iowans should dedicate the necessary resources and attention to the facility to assure its future as the showcase for Iowa agriculture, commerce, technology, and living arts that it has been for the past century."[38]

This essay returned the *Register* to its earlier role of fair booster, and Laird and the paper would continue cheering the efforts to refurbish this Iowa institution. Shortly after the column appeared, the board was putting the finishing touches on the foundation. Two others had been added to the fund-raising committee: Bill Riley, who had been involved with fair fund-raising since he came up with Fan Fair in 1988, and David Oman, a colleague of Riley's at Heritage Communications Inc. and former chief of staff for both Governors Robert Ray and Terry Branstad. That fall, the foundation was ready to go. But finding a director was not easy. Riley noted a "lack of top notch applicants for the funding job," and by the end of November 1991, the board was forced to alter its plans. It decided to stand pat, held off hiring a fund-raiser, and prepared a more conservative fund-raising campaign with Riley and Oman volunteering as chair and co-chair respectively.[39]

But the following month, board members changed their minds about hiring a foundation director. The shift occurred after a chance conversation between Robert (Bob) Schlutz and John Putney at the Association of Iowa Fairs' (AIF) annual meeting that December 1991. Schlutz had just been elected to the Iowa State Fair Board, and Putney, a farmer and cattleman from Gladbrook, a small town seventy miles northeast of Des Moines, had long been involved in the Iowa State Fair, first as an exhibitor then as president of the Sale of Champions and, as of 1990, beef superintendent. Politically savvy and well-connected, Putney was then the special assistant to Senator Chuck Grassley, a job he had held since 1989. Schlutz was also in the cattle business and had known Putney for years. When they saw each other at the AIF conference, they began talking about the Iowa State Fair. Putney asked Schlutz if he had seen the Rox Laird article and then said, "I hope the guys on the board are paying attention to what Rox said. He had the story right."[40]

Schlutz told Lucas and other board members of the conversation, and after brief discussion, the board thought Putney might be right for the fund-raiser job. Lucas called to gauge his interest, but Putney replied that he could not consider it because he had promised to remain on the Grassley staff through the upcoming 1992 election.[41]

So the board returned to its earlier plan of having a limited campaign. That spring, it rolled out its new foundation, cleverly named the Blue Ribbon Foundation, with the "Blue Ribbon Weekend" fund-raiser held at the fairgrounds over the Memorial Day holiday. The three days of festivities included the Rock and Roll Revue, a country music concert, World of Outlaws sprint car races, a camper and RV show, arts and crafts exhibits, horse shows, a 5-K run, and special events for children. While the weekend publicized the fairgrounds' great needs, Vaassen reported to the Fair Board that cold, rainy weather and competition from other holiday activities held down crowds, and the foundation lost $16,000 on the event.[42]

Fortunately, there were successes on other fronts. A September 1992 *Register* editorial praised Riley and Oman for raising over $100,000 through Fan Fest that year. But, as the paper reminded readers, that was "a drop in the bucket" considering the millions required for fairgrounds improvements. It continued: "Much of that will likely come from private and corporate donations but a good share of it by all rights should come from the state of Iowa. The fair is, after all, a state enterprise; it would be unconscionable for Iowa, which gains an enormous amount of free publicity and goodwill from the annual exposition, to ignore the fair in its time of need."[43]

The Fair Board understood the situation in a like manner. It was quietly seeking significant corporate contributions in advance of asking for state appropriations the following year, when it planned to mount a more extensive fund drive. For such a campaign, the board was again discussing the need for a full-time fund-raiser.

That fall 1992, Vaassen, Huinker, Lucas, and Governor Branstad solicited a large donation from Pioneer Hi-Bred International, one of the potential donors Braren had identified several years earlier. In November, a pleased Branstad told the Fair Board that Pioneer came through, pledging $500,000 toward the renovations of the Iowa State Fairgrounds if the board could raise $6 million, or 20 percent, of the $30 million goal over the next two calendar years. It was the largest single gift the fair had yet received. With the *Register* now clearly behind the board's efforts to restore the fair and a major gift now promised, Lucas thought their efforts had finally turned the corner. He played on the agricultural company's specific business when he explained the significance of the gift: "Now that Pioneer has planted the seed, we look forward to a great harvest."[44]

Deere & Company, another firm Braren had considered a prospective contributor to the fair, was next on the board's list of visits, but before approaching the company, it focused on hiring a full-time fund-raiser. The board had been moving slowly in that direction since July, but the

Pioneer challenge grant had increased the urgency. At the December 1992 board meeting, Huinker reported that the foundation subcommittee believed the time was right to hire the fund-raiser and wanted to go back to John Putney for the job. The board concurred.[45]

It was the right time for Putney as well. Senator Grassley had been re-elected the previous month, and the forty-eight-year-old political aide was thinking about a change. Lucas called Putney, who was indeed interested. The two visited the fairgrounds, dickered back and forth, and by the end of December, Putney accepted the position, which would begin in February 1993.[46]

The Blue Ribbon Foundation had been a long time in coming. In the early twentieth century, the Iowa State Fairgrounds had served the state and its citizenry remarkably well, but by midcentury, it was showing signs of its age. From then on, fair officials and board members began seeking solutions for the aging complex, but they could not find a fix. The money and the political will were just not there, and the neglected grounds fell into even greater disrepair. By 1992, however, it looked like the Fair Board and Marion Lucas had the right pieces in place. As the *Des Moines Register* explained that December, "The fund-raising foundation will become a permanent fixture and the plea for resources to rehabilitate the fairgrounds will be a familiar topic well into the next century." The Pioneer gift was a good start, but it also provided a stiff challenge: Could Putney and the Iowa State Fair Blue Ribbon Foundation raise the requisite $6 million over the next two years to access the seed corn company's money? And more importantly, could they reach their required $30 million goal to renovate the 107-year-old fairgrounds?[47]

Exposition Hall, shortly after
it was built, 1886. Courtesy
of the Iowa State Fair Blue
Ribbon Foundation.

Iowa State Fair, looking east up Grand Avenue. Exposition Hall is the
large building on the right, ca. 1890s. Courtesy of the Iowa State Fair
Blue Ribbon Foundation.

Iowa State Fair, looking south and east. Exposition Hall is up on the hill on the left, the Agriculture Building is below it, and the Livestock Pavilion is to the right, ca. 1905. Courtesy of the Iowa State Fair Blue Ribbon Foundation.

Pioneer Hall, the last remaining original structure built for the permanent fairground in 1886, in need of renovation, ca. 1980s. It was restored in 1996. Courtesy of the Iowa State Fair Blue Ribbon Foundation.

Grandfather's Barn is the only structure remaining from the Calvin
Thornton farm, which was purchased in 1885 to create the permanent Iowa
State Fairgrounds. The barn is pictured here after being renovated in 1994.
Courtesy of the Iowa State Fair Blue Ribbon Foundation.

Machinery Hall (now the William C. Knapp Varied Industries Building)
shortly after it was constructed in 1911. Courtesy of the Iowa State Fair Blue
Ribbon Foundation.

Steel Amphitheatre, State Fair Grounds, Des Moines, Iowa.
Length 380 feet. Depth 109 feet. Seats 8500 people.

The Grandstand, as it was originally built in 1909, before it was enlarged and its brick façade was added in 1927. Courtesy of the Iowa State Fair Blue Ribbon Foundation.

The Grandstand, pictured here in 2004, several years after being renovated in 1997. Courtesy of the Iowa State Fair.

Fairgoers resting on the wide porch of the popular Women's and
Children's Building, ca. 1915. The building was demolished in 1980
because funds for restoration could not be found. Courtesy of the Iowa
State Fair Blue Ribbon Foundation.

The popular Ye Old Mill float ride was built in 1920. Badly needed repairs
were planned but a windstorm leveled the building in 1996, requiring the
structure to be completely rebuilt that year, ca. 2000. Courtesy of the Iowa State
Fair Blue Ribbon Foundation.

52

Bill Riley, left, who hosted the Bill Riley Talent Search, stands with
several contestants and fair manager Kenny Fulk, ca. 1970. Courtesy of
the Iowa State Fair Blue Ribbon Foundation.

Don Greiman, at the time Fair Board president, with fair manager
Jim Taylor, 1980. Courtesy of Jim Taylor.

Governor Terry Branstad, seated, signs the Iowa State Fair Checkoff (the Corndog Checkoff) bill into law. Standing left to right are state representative Hubert Houser, who introduced the bill to the Iowa House, Beth Reinig (Greiner), assistant director of the foundation, and John Putney, 1993. Courtesy of the Iowa State Fair Blue Ribbon Foundation.

Fair manager Marion Lucas at the Blue Ribbon Foundation's kickoff of its "Treasure Our Fair" campaign, 1993. Note the limited edition prints of the artist Frank Murphy's "Champions on Parade" painting, which were auctioned off at the event. Courtesy of the Iowa State Fair Blue Ribbon Foundation.

Senator Chuck Grassley in the Blue Ribbon Foundation's merchandise booth, Iowa State Fair, 1993. Courtesy of the Iowa State Fair Blue Ribbon Foundation.

Artist Bill McNarney, second from left, did pen and ink drawings for the Blue Ribbon Foundation. With McNarney are John Putney and early foundation staff members Beth Reinig (Greiner) and Josette Schira (now Charboneau), 1994. Courtesy of the Iowa State Fair Blue Ribbon Foundation.

Engraved brick from the foundation's "Buy a Brick" giving program ready to be installed. Begun in 1994, the program allows fairgoers to have personal inscriptions etched on bricks and placed in various locations on the fairgrounds, 2015. Courtesy of the Iowa State Fair Blue Ribbon Foundation.

Advertisement for first limited edition model tractor sold by the Blue Ribbon Foundation, 1995. Courtesy of Beth (Reinig) Greiner.

The Agriculture Building under renovation, 1995. Courtesy of the Iowa State Fair Blue Ribbon Foundation.

Billboards such as this were donated by Universal Sign, Ragan Outdoor Advertising, and Hawkeye Advertising and promoted the Corndog Checkoff campaign in Des Moines, Iowa City, Cedar Rapids, and Mason City, 1996. Courtesy of the Iowa State Fair Blue Ribbon Foundation.

SHOT OUT OF A CANNON

4

Shortly before John Putney was hired, fair manager Marion Lucas told the *Des Moines Register*'s Rox Laird that with the full-time fund-raiser soon in place, he and the Fair Board hoped the Blue Ribbon Foundation could raise half of its $30 million goal over the remainder of the 1990s. He may have changed this rosy forecast, however, had he known that several days after Putney, who had only dabbled in raising money, took the position, he went into a Barnes & Noble store and bought all the books he could find on fund-raising. "I knew we'd had a false start with the foundation, and I wanted to be sure we got it right this time," Putney recalled, "so I read everything on fund-raising I could get my hands on."[1]

Actually, Lucas need not have worried; he and the board had made the right decision. Although on paper Putney did not fit the bill—his Iowa State University bachelor's degree was in farm operations, and his professional background was in the cattle business—he had an infectious love of the fair and was a natural politician who knew how to work with all kinds of people. What he lacked in fund-raising experience, he made up for with connections in the agricultural, business, and political world. And he had a vision of restoring this treasured fairgrounds, what he once called "the heart and soul of Iowa," which he easily conveyed to all comers. Maybe most important from the board's perspective, Putney recognized that the Iowa State Fair belonged to all Iowans, and buy-in was critical.

He knew it was vital to convince all Iowans, from farmers and small-town merchants in the countryside to executives and professionals in the cities, that the fair represented a major part of the state's past and present, and their help was required to preserve it for future generations. Such a show of broad support could lead to much needed legislative appropriations. Moving quickly was also important; $6 million had to be raised by the end of 1994 to get the $500,000 Pioneer

Hi-Bred International (now DuPont Pioneer) challenge grant. At the announcement of his hiring, Putney explained his plan in general terms: "I'm going to develop a campaign to be specific, attractive, and people-oriented and to develop our plan of attack with a sense of urgency." And with that, he and the renewed foundation blasted onto the scene with the speed and force of a human cannonball.[2]

Putney made three important moves before beginning the job in February. First, he, Lucas, and the board hashed out where the foundation would be housed. From the beginning, the board had planned on locating it at the fairgrounds in the Administration Building, although interestingly, there had also been talk of putting it in its present-day space in the Earth Home. Putney, however, thought it important that the foundation set up shop in downtown Des Moines, where he could meet and befriend the city's influential business and community leaders. This was essential because he understood "that this business of fund-raising is all about building relationships and credibility," and the foundation needed the financial support and goodwill of these movers and shakers. Some on the Fair Board chafed at the idea, but it carried the day. Board member Bob Schlutz remembered arguing that the foundation "needed to be downtown for a little while until such time as John [Putney] gets established because he's rubbin' shoulders with the people that are the ones that are gonna give." So the foundation rented space on the ninth floor of Two Ruan Center in the heart of the city's business district.[3]

Second, Putney hired an assistant, tapping the young Beth Reinig (now Greiner) for the job. Reinig had met Putney a couple of years earlier when she interned in Senator Chuck Grassley's Des Moines office. Shortly after graduating from Iowa State University in December 1990, she went on to manage Grassley's Washington, DC, office. Reinig returned to Iowa over the Christmas holiday in 1992 and touched base with Putney. He had always thought highly of her, and when Reinig said she was considering moving back to the Midwest, Putney told her of the Blue Ribbon Foundation and offered her the job as his assistant director.[4]

She took it, and soon the two were laying out the framework for their initial, two-year $6 million fund drive, appropriately named "Treasure Our Fair." At the same time, Putney and Reinig worked with CMF&Z Advertising to develop a logo, which would incorporate the then Iowa State Fair emblem, a marketing plan, and campaign materials. Meanwhile, Lucas and the Fair Board hoped to build on the interest the Pioneer gift had generated by seeking a second significant contribution; this time, they looked to Deere & Company, another firm targeted several years earlier by consultant Howard Braren.

Putney contacted Jerry Parkin, a longtime friend of the fair (he would be elected to the Fair Board in 2000) and director of state government affairs for Deere & Company, seeking a large donation from the equipment manufacturer to the fair. He also asked that Parkin arrange a visit for Governor Terry Branstad and Marion Lucas with Deere CEO Hans Becherer at the company headquarters in Moline, Illinois. (Actually, Lucas had approached Parkin several years earlier about getting his firm to provide John Deere tractors to pull the Iowa State Fair shuttles, which Deere & Company eventually did.) Parkin arranged the meeting, but a January ice storm forced its cancellation. A conference call took place instead, with Branstad and Lucas asking for a $1 million contribution.[5]

Becherer had known the two were seeking a donation but believed it would be in the $100,000 range, so he was caught by surprise. He called Parkin, who suggested the firm match Pioneer's pledge. Becherer ultimately agreed, and in late March, Governor Branstad proudly announced that the John Deere Foundation was providing a major boost for the fair, donating $500,000 toward the restoration of the Agriculture Building and Administration Building. If the Pioneer gift opened the door for the Blue Ribbon Foundation, the Deere gift gave the organization all-important momentum.[6]

As Deere & Company mulled over the gift, Putney met with Dennis Ryerson and Rox Laird of the *Des Moines Register*'s editorial page that February. He was well aware that the paper had been supportive of the fair and wanted it to continue, so he began cultivating a relationship with the two journalists. Ever since his passionate August 1991 op-ed plea to save the fairgrounds, Laird was clearly predisposed to back restoration efforts, and editorially, the paper remained in the Iowa State Fair's camp.[7]

By that time, Putney was going after money from a number of different sources. First was the legislature. While lobbying at the Iowa State Capitol, however, he was surprised to learn that a number of representatives did not realize the fair was a state-owned institution.

Therefore, as he pursued funding from the general assembly, Putney also spent a lot of time educating legislators about the fair, its history, and the badly needed renovations. This effort blossomed a couple of years later into the foundation's annual "Legislative Day at the Fair," where Putney and his staff hosted a luncheon for legislators during the last Thursday of the fair, provided them with a tour of the grounds, and publicly recognized them on the Plaza Stage (now the Bill Riley Stage).[8]

According to Fair Board member Paul Vaassen, Putney's first attempt to secure legislative funding for the fair was helped by the corporate gifts it had in hand. The new executive director argued that such support from prominent players in the state's agribusiness suggested the fair merited public support as well, and here he sought help on two different levels. Initially he dusted off an idea mentioned a couple of years earlier by David Oman: create an Iowa State Fair income tax checkoff, allowing state taxpayers to contribute to the fair fund-raising drive on their tax returns. This would be modeled after the successful "Chickadee Checkoff," which was established in 1981 and made it easy for Iowa taxpayers to support the Iowa Department of Natural Resources' fish and wildlife fund.[9]

Legislators were originally only lukewarm to the idea, but Putney kept pressing and negotiating. He convinced Hubert Houser, a first-year representative from western Iowa Putney had met while a Grassley aide when Houser was a member of the Pottawatomie County Board of Supervisors, to draft and sponsor the bill creating the fair checkoff. Houser did, while Putney kept telling representatives and senators of the critical needs of the fairgrounds, and the bill passed. Later dubbed the "Corndog Checkoff," the new law provided an easy way for everyday Iowans to contribute to the renovation of the fairgrounds, and the dollars rolled in. In the 1993 tax year, thousands of Iowans used the checkoff to give an average of over $6 each, raising $107,000 for the fair. The following year, these contributions rose to $128,000. Iowans have continued using the checkoff, donating a total of more than $1.7 million from their tax returns down to the present.[10]

Putney also pursued outright appropriations for the fairgrounds and found success here as well. The foundation received a $500,000 appropriation in 1993 and $1.5 million in Iowa Lottery profits over the next three years. Key legislators in securing the public money included Senators Tony Bisignano, Larry Murphy, Emil Husak, Berl Priebe, Leonard Boswell, Derryl McLaren, and Representatives Ron Corbett, Jack Beaman, Cliff Branstad, and Jim Hahn. Many of these figures remained stalwart supporters of the fair during their time in the legislature, but their actions were especially crucial this time around, providing Putney a quarter of the monies necessary to meet the Pioneer challenge and get its $500,000 check.[11]

The *Register* cheered the foundation's efforts to date, writing in May 1993 that the "Iowa State Fair is finally beginning to get some respect—and much-needed financial backing for building renovation." This was a good beginning, but the paper reminded readers that $30 million in work was needed and while the money should continue to come from a variety of sources, "It is critical that the Legislature make a serious, long-term commitment to rebuilding the fairgrounds. It is, after all, a state facility that serves an important function for all of Iowa."[12]

News of these early achievements bred another success. As Putney and Reinig were considering a gala to introduce the rejuvenated Blue Ribbon Foundation and the "Treasure Our Fair" campaign to the community, local restauranteur Jimmy Lynch had been reading about the fair's fund-raising arm and called with a serendipitous offer. He was preparing to open the swank 801 Steak & Chop House in the Principal skyscraper, 801 Grand, in downtown Des Moines. For the centerpiece of his livestock-themed décor, he had commissioned Frank Champion Murphy, the official artist of the American Angus Association, to do a painting for the restaurant. The renowned Iowa-born painter was inspired by images of events in the Livestock Pavilion at the Iowa State Fair, and his resulting work, "Champions on Parade," depicted a crowd inside the pavilion watching a cattle show in the 1920s.[13]

The painting gave Lynch an idea to help the foundation, which he expected would also attract good publicity for the new high-end eatery. First, he told Putney, he was willing to give Blue Ribbon Foundation rights to the prints and signed proofs of the painting, which it could use for fund-raising purposes. Second, he offered the foundation use of the restaurant the evening before its official scheduled opening for an event. Putney saw a great opportunity and took Lynch up on the proposal.[14]

Earlier, when Bill Riley and Oman chaired the foundation, they and the Fair Board had begun assembling an advisory board of significant business, community, and political leaders for the foundation— people whose names would attract attention and hopefully would contribute to the campaign. Putney made other additions, and as the kickoff neared, fifty-six leading Iowans were in the group, including Governor Branstad, former Governor Robert Ray, all of Iowa's congressional delegation, and Cooper Evans, former congressman and presidential agricultural advisor, who was named the honorary chairman of the "Treasure Our Fair" campaign. Among the others on the board were John Ruan, real estate developer Bill Knapp, Casey's General Stores CEO Don Lamberti, Pioneer CEO Tom Urban, newspaperman Michael Gartner, and Gary Kirke, head of the insurance firm Kirke-Van Orsdel.[15]

These dignitaries and a number of other prominent figures attended the June 1993 kickoff for the Iowa State Fair Blue Ribbon Foundation's "Treasure Our Fair" campaign. Held in the elegant new restaurant, the event featured a sumptuous dinner, speeches, an unveiling of the "Champions on Parade" painting, and an auction for some numbered proofs and signed prints of the painting. The number one artist proof was auctioned off for $10,000 to foundation board member John Hagie, CEO of Hagie Manufacturing, a maker of farm equipment, who joked with Jerry Parkin that the purchase had saved his company $490,000, a reference to the recent Deere & Company gift.[16]

Des Moines Register farm editor Don Muhm was impressed with the kickoff, writing that the evening got the fair's fund-raising campaign "off to a booming start." The event proved another early success for the foundation, giving it positive buzz among Des Moines's movers and shakers. It was also here that Putney let donors and potential donors know that the fair and foundation would go out of their way to recognize the generosity of individual and corporate supporters. Putney became widely known for telling colleagues and Fair Board members that, "we should always give donors more than they expect." He made this clear during the kickoff, when the foundation presented special artist proofs of the "Champions on Parade" painting to Pioneer Hi-Bred and Deere & Company in appreciation for their lead gifts.[17]

With the Pioneer gift, the John Deere donation, and the successful kickoff gala, Putney was feeling good about the foundation's prospects. "Things were moving along nicely," he recalled, "then the flood of 1993 hit, and I thought that was it; we weren't going to raise any more money." The mid-July floods brought Des Moines to a standstill, and for two weeks the city was without water. Although travel in and around central Iowa was difficult, a depressed Putney went to check his mail, and after a much longer than usual drive, he got into his office. There waiting for him was a letter with a check for $30,000. The donation was from Sandra Dowie, whose family owned the Freeman Company, a Des Moines-based event planning and trade show firm. The gift could not have come at a better time; it lifted Putney's spirits and renewed his belief in the foundation's future. He made every effort to thank and recognize Dowie for the contribution, and the gift only strengthened his belief in the importance of "giving donors more than they expect."[18]

This conviction was one of the reasons Putney and his wife, Emily, decided to stay at the fairgrounds beginning with the 1993 fair. He chose to put their trailer just east of the Livestock Pavilion (soon renamed the Pioneer Livestock Pavilion in honor of the seed company's major gift) near the campsite he had used while serving as beef superintendent. Although a central location, it was unkempt, with a hodgepodge of old trailers and campers. Putney pushed the Fair Board to clean up this section of the fairgrounds, and he created a Blue Ribbon Foundation hospitality area adjacent to his fifth-wheel camper, which he persuaded Don Moore, co-owner of Twin Anchors RV in Colo, a small town forty-five miles northeast of Des Moines, to donate to the Blue Ribbon Foundation for use during the fair.[19]

Here in the hospitality area Putney entertained benefactors and potential benefactors. The foundation made incremental improvements to its compound until 2004, when Conrad Clement, head of Featherlite Inc., told Putney, "If you grade this area and level it out, I'll bring in a luxury motor coach for your use during the fair." With that, the executive director coaxed Des Moines-based contractor McAninch to grade the campground gratis and then asked his son to build a retaining wall and landscape the compound. As promised, Clement provided a grand mobile home for the Putneys' use during the fair. Besides visiting with people at the hospitality tent, Putney often whisked them away on golf cart tours of the fairgrounds, highlighting the needs of the aging facility. And to make large donors' stay at the Iowa State Fair a little nicer, the foundation soon provided them with convenient complimentary parking immediately east of its hospitality tent.[20]

Putney continued working the big donor circuit, where he succeeded in matching large corporate gifts to specific projects. His first concern was Grandfather's Barn, the only remaining building on the fairgrounds from the original farmstead purchase. It had been closed for safety reasons since 1989, and Putney felt strongly that restoring and reopening the building would boost morale for fair staffers and fairgoers alike. He went to Lois Vermeer, head of the foundation of the Vermeer Company, a manufacturer of agricultural and industrial equipment in Pella, a small town forty miles southeast of Des Moines, and told her the story of the barn and its significance to the fair. Vermeer came through with a $100,000 gift to restore the building.[21]

Shortly thereafter, Boatmen's Bank (now Bank of America) responded to Putney's request with a $100,000 pledge and was "thrilled to be a participant in restoring" the historic Ye Old Mill amusement ride to its original 1920s condition. Firstar Bank (now U.S. Bank) met the call and donated $100,000 toward a new service center, which would be located between the Administration Building and the Varied Industries Building and include automated teller machines (ATMs), a first-aid facility, an information booth, and telephones. This was followed by Farm Bureau's contribution of more than $245,000 for the restoration of Pioneer Hall. Other large donors included Casey's General Stores, the Principal Financial Group, and Midwest Resources (now MidAmerican Energy), whose former CEO was Putney's brother, Mark Putney.[22]

Not all of Des Moines's leaders were supportive of the foundation's efforts, however. Some key figures viewed its fund-raising as competition and feared it might siphon off money that would otherwise be devoted to the city's downtown projects. A prominent Des Moines attorney who was very active in the Greater Des Moines Chamber of Commerce (now the Greater Des Moines Partnership) confronted Putney early on, saying, "What are you trying to do? We don't need a battle over Des Moines dollars. They belong downtown." Des Moines city councilman

Archie Brooks lodged a similar complaint. But Putney, who was fiercely passionate about the fair and its restoration efforts, responded to each with the same short, determined reply, "I'm going to do what I have to do [to raise money for the fair]."[23]

Putney and the foundation continued seeking big dollars from corporations and wealthy individuals, but they did not forget to involve everyday Iowans in their effort to restore the fair. To that end, they developed opportunities for individuals to give at a variety of levels. Shortly after Putney was named director, Bill McNarney, manager for the US Department of Housing and Urban Development in Iowa, offered what Putney considered "the first gift to the foundation." The two had become acquainted when Putney worked for Grassley. McNarney said he did not have any money to contribute, but he was a talented artist, known for sketching local landmarks such as the covered bridges, barns, and colleges, and proposed to do fourteen pen-and-ink drawings of the major buildings at the fairgrounds for the Blue Ribbon Foundation, which could sell reproductions on notecards, calendars, and mugs. The illustrations debuted on various souvenirs in 1993 and are still sold by the foundation today. Putney called the McNarney prints "an invaluable source of fund-raising and promotion for our cause." Such merchandise, as well as commemorative pins, hats, T-shirts, tote bags, and the like, became a critical source of revenue for the foundation, and by 1994 its merchandise booth had netted over $50,000.[24]

Putney was also thinking about other ways to tie individuals to the fair. He was full of ideas, Beth (Reinig) Greiner remembered. "He used to drive from his home in Gladbrook [seventy miles northeast of Des Moines] into Des Moines every day and would come in with these fabulous ideas. He had a little tape recorder, and he would talk into his recorder and then come in and play it back and write down the ideas. He wasn't afraid to come up with ideas and bring them to light."[25]

One such idea that Putney dusted off was a commemorative brick program, which had been discussed by fair officials for some time but never been initiated. People could purchase bricks at $75 each, have them inscribed with the name of a family member, a deceased relative, or just a special memory, and then installed in one of five "Walk of Memories" pathways at the fair, in the campground, or in front of the Cattle, Horse,

Sheep, or Swine Barns. The program gave individual small donors a way to invest in the fair and receive recognition similar to big corporate contributors' naming rights to buildings. As fairgoer Kevin West, who had a brick inscribed for his wife, put it, "The thing about seeing the brick is that it's like a shot of immortality."[26]

Brick sales started in the winter of 1994 and were immensely popular. By the following summer, the foundation had raised $175,000 through the program, which continues to be a good money raiser today. It also led to other similar ideas for Iowans to invest in their fairgrounds' restoration. "Trees Fair-ever" was announced in 1995, though it was almost immediately rechristened "Trees for the Fair" because the nonprofit organization Trees Forever felt the name resembled its moniker too closely. For $100, a tree would be planted on the grounds, and the donor would be recognized on a plaque in the Administration Building. The following year, Putney added the "Have a Seat" program: for $325, an individual or group could buy a park bench, which would include a prominently displayed donor plaque. As with the bricks, these fund-raising opportunities were popular, improved the fairgrounds, and gave contributors their own little corner of the facility.[27]

A year before the brick program, Putney had come across a potential source of funding, although it seemed like a long shot. Shortly after he started with the foundation, he, Vaassen, and Lucas went to Washington, DC, to investigate federal programs that might provide funds for the fairgrounds. It was here Putney learned of the Intermodal Surface Transportation Efficiency Act of 1991 (ISTEA), which made the US Department of Transportation (DOT) a possible funder. Under this law, 10 percent of federal highway money sent to each state was to be used toward "transportation enhancements." After returning to Washington and visiting with federal DOT officials in June 1993, Putney believed he could make the case to get such funding for the fairgrounds, and the Iowa State Fair Board voted to seek $6 million in ISTEA monies for renovation of the Grandstand.[28]

Putney and Reinig put together several different proposals trying to link the fairgrounds to transportation improvements as a justification to tap into ISTEA funds but were repeatedly turned down. In the midst of applying, they lowered their request by nearly half and finally emphasized that the fair was a transportation destination, with Iowa Highway 163 (East University Avenue), which ran along the north side of the fairgrounds, being used to bring livestock and patrons to the annual exhibition. As for the Grandstand, it was located on the Grand Concourse and had been central to major public programs at the fairgrounds since 1909.[29]

Their persistence paid off. In July 1994 the Des Moines Area Metropolitan Planning Organization, which had $2.5 million of federal transportation improvement money to distribute, gave the fair $500,000 toward the Grandstand renovation. Two months later, the Iowa Department of Transportation allocated $750,000 of its ISTEA money for the Grandstand as well. These decisions were controversial, however, because opponents failed to see the connection between the Grandstand and the enhancement of transportation. Then the US Department of Transportation stepped in and refused to send the money through to the fair because a recent federal highway memorandum stated that such grants needed to show a "substantial relationship to transportation," which the Blue Ribbon Foundation's proposal did not. Putney was incensed, believing the rules of the game had been changed midstream. He went to Washington, DC, and talked with members of the Iowa congressional delegation. Grassley pushed for the decision to be reviewed, and the federal DOT reversed itself, announcing the following June that the fair would receive the money because the grants had already been approved by the appropriate state and local agencies.[30]

While he worked behind the scenes to get these grants reinstated, Putney also understood the importance of keeping the Blue Ribbon Foundation's story and its successes before the public. He and Reinig spent a lot of time with various service and civic groups speaking about the fair, its renovation needs, and the foundation. These presentations were often accompanied by a short video they made entitled "Treasure Our Fair" narrated by local radio and television personality Mike Pace. Reinig also talked up the campaign on the airways, frequently going out on weeklong media tours where she made the rounds on local radio stations throughout the state. But Putney knew this was not enough, and in early 1994, he added a full-time communication director to the staff, hiring recent Drake graduate Josette Schira (now Charboneau). She immediately began working on a foundation newsletter.[31]

The *Blue Ribbon* was first published in spring 1994 and came out quarterly thereafter. It gave updates on the foundation's fund-raising and what those dollars were doing for the fairgrounds, provided short profiles of individual donors, described new programs, thanked each and every person who contributed, and asked for readers' continued support. Through this newsletter, other media outlets, and a friendly relationship with the *Des Moines Register*, Putney adeptly told the story of the fair and its needs. He had an uncanny ability to connect with a wide variety of constituencies, and as Judy Nye, an education professor, founder of the Iowa State Fair singers, and later a fund-raiser at Luther College, explained, "Putney could reach those in the farmyard and those in the boardroom." Furthermore, and essential to fund-raising, Nye added, "The foundation did an especially good job of publicizing its success by making the fairgrounds' improvements visible and showing people where their dollars were going."[32]

An early success certainly worth touting came in October 1994, when a couple months ahead of schedule, the foundation announced it had met the Pioneer Hi-Bred challenge to raise $6 million by the end of that year. To date, the "Treasure Our Fair" campaign had amassed $6.9 million in pledges, gifts, and in-kind services. Putney was delighted, but clearly wanted to keep all eyes on the long-term $30 million goal. He explained, "This is just the first step toward projecting our Fairgrounds into the 21st century. We have many exciting projects underway and many more up and coming renovations through the end of the century; we have only just begun to tap the surface."[33]

The *Register* was pleased as well, noting in an editorial headlined, "Pitching in for the Fair" that over $2 million of the total raised had come from individuals. "That's just the way the money ought to be raised," it wrote. "The State Fair belongs to every Iowan, and the fairgrounds and annual State Fair are important fixtures in memories for many; everyone ought to have the opportunity to help preserve the fair for future generations." But, like Putney, it reminded readers, "While the first goal of $6 million has been met, the Blue Ribbon Foundation has a long way to go before its work is done."[34]

By 1994, fairgoers could see the beginnings of improvements. A completely renovated Vermeer's Grandfather's Barn reopened the first day of the fair after being closed for five years, and the fairgrounds received a general sprucing up. Sewers were replaced, streets were repaved, new sidewalks were poured, restrooms were added, and new lighting was installed. The Sheep Barn got a badly needed new roof, renovation began on the Administration Building, and the Agriculture Building underwent a major face-lift, getting a new roof, windows, doors, and brick and mortar repairs. This last structure was renamed the John Deere Agriculture Building in honor of the corporation's large gift. Construction also commenced on the Firstar Service Center, which opened for the 1995 fair. Besides being the first new building erected with funds raised by the foundation, the service center was fully heated and air conditioned, making it available for year-round use. This was an important factor in future building restoration and new construction as the Fair Board and officials looked to develop the fairgrounds' off season meeting, convention, and exhibition business.[35]

But no work had yet taken place on the deteriorating Grandstand. Actually, at one point, some members of the Fair Board considered replacing the aging edifice with a big-box auditorium for major events and concerts. Putney fought against taking down the stately signature structure, arguing: "If you do that, I will have a difficult time with my fund-raising. When you've got buildings like the Grandstand and the Agriculture Building and the Sheep Barn, all of which are considered some of the outstanding exposition-style buildings in the United States, they should be preserved." His position carried the day, and the foundation soon secured $1.25 million in ITSEA funds for the Grandstand's restoration, but by then estimates for its repair had reached $9 million.[36]

In the winter of 1995, Lucas and Putney went to the legislature for a big appropriation, $15 million over five years. The successful early closing out of the "Treasure Our Fair" challenge campaign and the widespread support the foundation had received from individuals and corporations, coupled with clear evidence that the dollars were making a difference at the fairgrounds, gave the two plenty of ammunition to address the Iowa General Assembly. Thanks to strong support of representatives such as Iowa General Assembly Speaker Ron Corbett, Majority Leader Brent Siegrist, Mike Cataldo, Chuck Gipp, and Dave Millage, as well as Senators Tony Bisignano, Rod Halvorson, Larry Murphy, Leonard Boswell, and Don Gettings, the fair received generous funding, although as discussions ensued, the amount was whittled down to $9 million. On the upside, it was a lump sum for the 1996 fiscal year. Designated for capital improvements at the fairgrounds, the money came from lottery revenue and the Iowa Infrastructure Fund.[37]

As if celebrating this success, the world premiere of a new stage musical based on Rodgers and Hammerstein's "State Fair" opened at the Des Moines Civic Center that August. The show starred well-known actors John Davidson and Kathryn Crosby as Abel and Melissa Frake, and Andrea McArdle and Ben Wright as their children, Margy and Wayne. It was an immediate hit in Iowa. *Register* critic Joan Bunke called the show "Heartland hokum at its best," writing, "it is old-fashioned first-class stage fun," while *Variety*, the show business daily, noted, "The producers of this wholesome familial celebration had the savvy to combine its Des Moines launch in August with the real Iowa State Fair, attracting much ink and charming the pants off assorted urban scribes unused to cavorting on Midwestern midways." After its ten-day run in Des Moines, "State Fair" went on an eight-month national tour before heading to Broadway.[38]

But Putney and the foundation had to push on. Several months before the show opened, they held May Fair '95, a benefit cocktail party and silent auction in conjunction with Very Special Arts Iowa, a nonprofit organization designed to encourage those with mental and physical challenges to engage in the arts, now a state entity known as VSA Iowa. The two organizations already had a relationship as Very Special Arts held its annual Governor's Very Special Arts Festival on the Fun Forest Stage during the fair (this event continues today and is known as VSA Iowa Presents). While in the midst of planning a fund-raiser, Sue Jensen, the director of Very Special Arts, contacted Jan Higgins, assistant manager of the fair, about co-sponsoring the event. She talked to Lucas, who discussed it with the foundation. Reinig thought it a great idea and suggested holding the benefit at the Iowa Tourism Building (now the Elwell Family Food Center) at the fairgrounds, which would give the foundation and fair a higher profile. Thus the first May Fair party and auction, held on May Day, was born.[39]

With local television news personalities Ed Wilson and Laurie Groves hosting the program, the 1995 Very Special Arts/Blue Ribbon Foundation benefit went well; more than 150 people attended the event, which raised $13,000. All involved were pleased, and planning began for a second joint benefit auction the following year.[40]

This and its seemingly ever-expanding activities suggested the foundation needed more help, but rather than look to another full-time staffer, Putney offered two internships to college students, beginning in the summer of 1995. The interns assisted with special events, updated data bases, helped coordinate volunteers during the fair, and worked on marketing and promotions. And as the foundation's programs grew, two more interns were eventually added.[41]

Another key change at the 1995 exhibition went largely unnoticed by fairgoers. Several years earlier, Tom Heiken, owner of Crystal Clear Water, began selling bottled water at the fair from a small booth on Grand Avenue. "Other vendors," Heiken remembered, "questioned why we would sell bottled water with all of the beer and pop sales throughout the grounds. To our surprise the bottled water became very popular." As water sales grew over the next couple of years, Marion Lucas told Putney he thought the foundation should take over the sales at the fair. When Putney responded that this would put Heiken out of business, Lucas suggested Heiken might act as the exclusive wholesaler of water to the foundation. The foundation in turn would be the sole distributor of water to vendors wishing to sell it at the fair as well as retail water to fairgoers at its own stand.[42]

Heiken was amenable, but before inking the agreement, Putney explained that the foundation would hold a blind taste test of various bottled waters. When Mountain Valley Spring Water, the green-bottled brand Heiken carried, won the contest, the two signed the deal. There were some initial bumps in the road, however. That first year was especially hot, and Reinig and Putney had not ordered enough water for the fair. They ran out after only two days, and because the bottled water came from Arkansas, they had to scramble to replace it until another shipment could arrive. Beyond that misstep, some fair vendors grumbled that if they wished to carry water, they had to go through the foundation to buy it, but the issue soon died down as concessionaires came to view it as a cost of doing business at the fair.[43]

The move proved lucrative. Bottled water sales raised over $36,000 for the foundation in 1995, and by 1998, the concession had netted $100,000. From there, the foundation branched out, increasing the number of its fairground water stands from one to six, and by 2014, it was selling over 240,000 bottles of water every year at the fair, adding $175,000 to the foundation's coffers annually.[44]

One reason water sales were so successful was low overhead; the stands were staffed almost entirely by volunteers. Volunteers had been important to the foundation from the beginning, first operating its merchandise booth, then selling bottled water and helping with a variety of other activities. Beth (Reinig) Greiner considered volunteers the foundation's "secret weapon," allowing the "David"-sized organization to tackle the "Goliath of a goal" of preserving the fairgrounds.[45]

Over the years, more and more volunteers were needed as the foundation added new programs, and Iowans continued stepping up. By 2015, the work of 563 Blue Ribbon volunteers helped generate over $570,000 for the foundation. Of this crew, one person—Margo Fox—stood out, widely acknowledged as its leading volunteer. She met her husband-to-be at the fair in 1989 and married him there three years later. In appreciation for letting her have her wedding on the grounds, Fox volunteered for the fair's Bill Riley Talent Search in 1992, and the following year she was recruited by the foundation, making her its "original volunteer." Fox has continued donating her time to the foundation ever since, setting up concession stands, selling water and fair souvenirs, shuttling fairgoers around the grounds, and chairing the party and auction committees for the foundation's annual fund-raiser.[46]

Meanwhile, that fall of 1995, just after the foundation first ventured into water sales, it introduced a new promotion. Putney had seen a special edition model tractor at a trade show and thought something similar would sell well for the foundation. He asked Parkin if Deere & Company (which, since its deal with Marion Lucas to provide tractors for the fair shuttles made it the official tractor of the Iowa State Fair) might give the foundation exclusive rights to sell a model depiction of one of its tractors. Parkin thought it a good idea and went to Don Margenthaler, head of the John Deere Foundation, who oversaw branding. He talked it over with other executives, who agreed, as long as Deere & Company could approve the final model and design. Putney then approached Ertl, a toymaker in the northeastern Iowa town of Dyersville, best known for die-cast metal models of vehicles and farm equipment, to do the work. The result was a one-sixteenth scale model of the John Deere 4440 tractor. Only 3,500 of these limited edition pieces were made, each laser etched with the tractor's serial number, the foundation name and logo, and the fair's logo embossed on the tractor's battery box. They went on sale in November 1995 for $75 each, or $150 if one wanted to purchase a specific numbered model tractor.[47]

The collectable tractors sold quickly. There were only five hundred remaining by the following spring, and they sold out during the fair. This led the foundation to team up with Ertl and John Deere several times over the next fifteen years, producing four more limited edition model tractors. As Putney had hoped, many collectors were eager to purchase (and pay extra for the privilege) the same serial number of the latest edition of their earlier tractor models. The success of the limited-run model tractors led the foundation to develop and sell a number of other restricted special edition items, such as commemorative pins, pottery pieces, and "Fairopoly," a limited edition Iowa State Fair version of the popular board game "Monopoly."[48]

In November 1995 the foundation launched its second fund-raising effort, a $7 million drive called "Rebuilding the Dream." Putney observed, "The support Iowa companies and individuals expressed with the first capital campaign—'Treasure Our Fair'—was exactly what we needed. Now it is critical that the momentum and the facility improvements continue. The 'Rebuilding the Dream' campaign is designed to do just that....With statewide support, we will reach our goal ensuring that the Iowa State Fair will continue to be the grand showcase of Iowa, her people, and her products."[49]

The campaign got off to a solid start with two substantial gifts. The first donation was spurred by the Fair Board, which was looking to replace an often muddy dirt road that ran up the hillside to a National Guard park between the Agriculture Building and the Livestock Pavilion with a pedestrian walkway and park. Lucas suggested this might be a project that Putney could sell to a corporate sponsor. The foundation's executive director agreed and thought the Pella Corporation, the window and door manufacturer based in Pella, might be interested. Soon he was talking with company CEO Wayne Bevis and his assistant, Mary Van Zante. He then entertained them at the Blue Ribbon Foundation compound at the fairgrounds, took them to the area that needed improvement, and showed them drawings of the proposed walkway. Putney concluded by telling them the fair could name the park Pella Plaza.[50]

Bevis and Van Zante saw the need and were impressed with the pitch, and the Pella Corporation donated $100,000 toward the 50,000-square-foot park, which would include water fountains, benches, trees and flowers, and flags representing all of Iowa's ninety-nine counties.[51]

Bill Riley, Mr. State Fair himself, pledged $100,000 as well, designating his funds toward the renovation of the Plaza Stage, where he had been introducing young Iowa talent at the fair for decades. With the 1996 fair his last to host the program, he explained the gift: "The Iowa State Fair has been a wonderful, exciting part of our family's life through the past fifty years. Anne [Riley's wife] and I feel we should try to give back in a small way for all that we have enjoyed through the years."[52]

Evidence of the foundation's success was becoming more and more visible at the fairgrounds, and the relationship Putney had built with Rox Laird of the *Register*'s editorial page continued paying dividends as the writer kept close tabs on the progress at the fairgrounds. The paper's lead editorial on July 14, 1996, commented: "Work was in full swing at the Iowa State Fairgrounds last week. The air was filled with the crack of hammers and the whine of power saws and the fragrance of fresh paint; the grounds were swarming with laborers pouring concrete, planting trees, and putting finishing touches on new landscaping. But this work is not so much in preparation for the 1996 edition of the Iowa State Fair...as for state fairs for future generations of Iowans." It then summarized the many upgrades and renovations on the grounds.[53]

Perhaps most important was the Grandstand, which had just undergone a $2.5 million restoration. Crumbling bricks and stonework were replaced, windows repaired, and new doors, a new roof, and new seating were installed. As more money was raised, the second phase of the renovation went forward, and the completely overhauled Grandstand was finished two years later.[54]

Other significant work included the fully rebuilt Ye Old Mill, the oldest ride at the fair, a renovation of the Plaza Stage, appropriately renamed the Bill Riley Stage, featuring an enlarged stage covered by an expansive roof. Following extensive work on its footings and foundation, a freshly painted Pioneer Hall also reopened, one hundred ten years after it first did in 1886. The attractive new Pella Plaza opened that year as well.[55]

A few months prior to the 1996 fair, Putney came up with another way to give back to donors as the foundation launched what became an annual golf event designed to thank major capital contributors. Putney arranged for Cecil Rueter, a farm equipment dealer in Grand Junction, a small town sixty-five miles northwest of Des Moines, to open his private golf course and home for the day. There the foundation provided a fun day of golf, prizes, and food for attendees, which included legislators, representatives for corporate donors, and private individuals.[56]

One notable businessman not there was Bill Knapp. He had not yet given anything significant to the fair, but Putney was actively courting him. The two had met a couple of years earlier in 1994. It was the last day of the Iowa State Fair, and Putney was having breakfast at the Dinner Bell, a popular eating spot at the northwest end of the Swine Barn, when he saw Knapp and his companion Susan Terry (the two would eventually marry in 1998) walk by. He recognized Knapp, jumped up and introduced himself, and then offered the two a golf cart tour of the fairgrounds. This began what would become a close friendship between Putney and Knapp.[57]

As the two became better friends over the next couple of years, Putney took every opportunity to take Knapp around the fairgrounds, tell him the illustrative history of the fair, and describe the foundation's plans to restore the historic site. By 1996, he knew Knapp was interested in the fair and sensed the time was right to ask for his support. Putney also thought he had the right project in mind—the Varied Industries Building. While in the midst of the Grandstand renovation, the Fair Board had looked to this 1911 structure as the next one in need of an update. In this case, the plan was to enclose the facility and heat and cool it, making it an attractive exhibition hall for year-round use.

Late that fall, Putney went to Knapp's office and made his pitch. He asked the business leader to make a commitment to the Iowa State Fair's effort to remodel the Varied Industries Building. Knapp wanted to know the dollar amount Putney had in mind. When he said $1 million, Knapp replied that he was thinking more in the range of $200,000. But Putney stayed the course. He knew a large gift from Knapp would draw a lot of attention and likely attract other donations to the foundation. So Putney responded, "Bill, I want yours to be the biggest gift in the history of the Iowa State Fair. And you do a lot for Des Moines and central Iowa, but this is for the whole state."[58]

Knapp liked the idea of expanding his giving beyond the city, and ever since he had been seeing Susan Terry, who had a long love of the fair, he had been drawn to the annual exhibition as well. Much as Putney had hoped, Knapp soon made the $1 million commitment, at the time the largest private donation to the fair. At the announcement in February 1997, Knapp explained, "When you're successful, you owe some of that back. I've been involved in a lot of things in the greater Des Moines area, but I've always wanted to do something for the state."[59]

Shortly after Knapp's pledge, Susan Terry called Putney and said that she and Bill wanted to camp at that year's upcoming fair. Spots at the campground were reserved long in advance, and shoehorning Knapp and Terry into a campsite was nearly impossible, but Putney was determined to show the foundation's appreciation. He found a campsite and lined up an old motor home for them. Knapp and Terry delighted in staying at the fair and began inviting influential friends for parties at their campsite.[60]

Knapp's gift and his camping at the fairgrounds would prove a game changer for the Blue Ribbon Foundation, marking the beginning of an even brighter future for the Iowa State Fair. Since being jump-started in 1993, the foundation had enjoyed great success. Putney had worked quickly to make connections, build relationships, and develop a wide range of giving programs. He had conveyed his passion for the fair and the urgent restoration needs in a manner that appealed to a broad spectrum of Iowans. By July 1996, he and the foundation had already raised more than $22.6 million, blowing past the goal Marion Lucas had set at the foundation's outset of raising $15 million over the course of the 1990s.[61]

The following summer, the foundation was nearing the original total goal of $30 million. The *Des Moines Register* appreciated how the Fair Board was using these funds at the fairgrounds: "What's notable…is that most of these improvements are not immediately recognizable. Instead of dropping big chucks of the nearly $30 million raised by the State Fair Blue Ribbon Foundation on glitzy new projects, the Fair Board has wisely invested the money in restoring the existing structures in a way that is faithful to their history and original design. That can be more expensive in many cases than new construction, but the Fair Board's goal is to preserve the Iowa State Fair, not to build a new one. That is wise policy, and Iowans can see the fruits of their donations to this effort beginning today [opening of 1997 fair]."[62]

But Putney and his team were only getting started. They had laid a solid foundation over their first few years, and now with the Knapp gift and his support, the future seemed assured. So much so, in fact, that over the next fifteen years the Iowa State Fair enjoyed a renaissance rivaling its golden age nearly a century earlier, when most of its grand buildings now being saved were originally constructed.

"OUR STATE FAIR IS A
GREAT STATE FAIR" REDUX

5

The Blue Ribbon Foundation's first four years restored the fortunes of the Iowa State Fair, but the next sixteen put it on an entirely new trajectory. With real estate tycoon Bill Knapp on board, John Putney began prying the big money coffers open, and he, the Fair Board, and the fair manager now had the opportunity to think on a much grander scale than merely restoring the grounds to their former glory. They could reinvent the fairgrounds, making it an outstanding year-round facility designed to meet the needs of Iowans in the coming century.

By 2007, Rox Laird, the *Des Moines Register*'s longtime fair watcher and advocate, penned an opinion piece praising the foundation's achievements. Over its fourteen-year existence, it had raised an astounding $65 million in public and private funds for the rebuilding of the fairgrounds. Meanwhile, Laird noted, "Across the nation, some state fairs have fallen on hard times. Iowa's fair, by contrast, has undergone a massive renovation project that is updating the fairgrounds for 21st century crowds and uses." Most fair buildings had been "carefully restored or replaced," and "around the classic fixtures—the Grandstand, the Agriculture Building, the Livestock Building—new buildings have been added, walks and grounds improved, and many new trees and benches installed." He summarized: "In short, the place was falling apart before the Blue Ribbon Foundation was created. Today, it is a showcase for the best of Iowa."[1]

Other states took notice. In 2001, for instance, a front page story in the *Omaha World-Herald* observed that "state fairs in Nebraska and Iowa are as different as a plain donut and a sugar-powdered funnel cake." While the paper noted that the exhibition in Nebraska was struggling, it called Iowa's "a national model for success," explaining that the fairgrounds had been "neglected and crumbling" until the Blue Ribbon Foundation was formed. Then things changed, the *World-Herald* reported, when,

"Like a barker at a carnival, Putney and his group hawk[ed] money from anyone, anywhere," and the fairgrounds' renaissance began. Soon Putney and Iowa State Fair Board members and officials were being asked by other state fair managers about the secrets to their success. They were also invited to make presentations on the foundation's magic formula at the annual Las Vegas convention of the International Association of Fairs and Expositions (IAFE).[2]

Putney remembered that other state fair administrators were never satisfied with the answers Iowa State Fair personnel provided. "They were all looking for some secret," he recalled, "but there wasn't one. So I'd tell them our success was based on hard work, some thought, and building relationships, which was critical."[3]

While many remained convinced there was a silver bullet solution that could resuscitate their fairs, Putney stuck to his three principles with great effect. There were problems and scuffles, of course, and disagreements and setbacks, but he and the foundation enjoyed amazing success, providing the Fair Board the wherewithal to revive the Iowa State Fairgrounds. By 2010, such activity was capped off with the completion of the Richard O. Jacobson Exhibition Center, a first-class arena aimed at attracting national and international horse and livestock shows.

The year 1997 brought important transitions for the foundation. Besides Knapp opening his wallet, the foundation received another large contribution, increased its control over fair fund-raising, and launched two new programs, all while experiencing a change in personnel.

A couple of months before Knapp's $1 million pledge became the largest private contribution to the fair, the foundation announced that it had been willed the estates of the Berneice and Donald Penningroth and his brother Orville. The brothers, residents of Wellman, a small town 115 miles east of Des Moines, were farmers who had exhibited shorthorn cattle and Poland China hogs at the Iowa State Fair since 1926. Putney was thrilled and explained, "The gift [ultimately totaling $470,000] goes well beyond its monetary value. It establishes the continuation of our State Fair tradition as a worthy cause of substantial bequests."[4]

Word of the fair's financial need was getting out, and although Putney was pleased, he still wanted greater involvement from the Des Moines community. To that end, he and Beth Reinig (now Greiner) began to reevaluate May Fair, their fund-raiser with Very Special Arts Iowa, after their second joint event in spring 1996 netted each group only $7,500. Reinig thought it was a lot of work with little return and suggested the foundation pursue its own fund-raising event. Putney concurred and invited Joyce Lock and Dee Wittmack, two longtime fair volunteers who were well connected in Des Moines society, to a brainstorming session. Lock and Wittmack agreed that a sole fund-raiser was the way to go and were interested in participating. Putney named them co-chairs of a volunteer committee to arrange the event. When he asked what the benefit should be called, Lock immediately proposed the "Corndog Kickoff." All liked the name, which played on one of the fair's iconic food items, and planning for the foundation's new fund-raiser began.[5]

By February 1997, Lock and Wittmack had laid out the broad structure of the event. The pre-fair event would be held that summer. There would be fair food to sample, a silent and live auction, music and dancing, topped off by rides in the fair's sky glider and fireworks. To organize the benefit gala, they filled the Corndog Kickoff committee with other prominent Des Moines figures. Meredith Watters, Allison Fleming, Jackie Gay, Sharon Granzow, Linda Hanson, Rick Hickman, Lenny Ramsey, and Karen Worth made up the auction subcommittee; Susan Terry (now Knapp), Rosalie Gallagher, Lana Jones Gould, Suzie Jones, Ruth Pearson, and Dixie Rhiner served on the party subcommittee; and Linda Ruble worked with Blue Ribbon communication managers Josette Schira (now Charboneau) and then Emily Reis (now Abbas), on publicity.[6]

A relatively modest goal of raising $10,000 was set for the event. Putney explained his objective to an early meeting of the committee: "Our goal is greater visibility. I don't really care if we make money." But Susan Terry would have none of this. "What are you talking about? Of course we're going to make money." And they did, far exceeding their goal.[7]

On July 18, an especially hot and muggy Friday evening, the Corndog Kickoff Benefit Auction and Fair Food Grazing Party took place in Pioneer Hall. A large crowd of 460 people turned out and were met by official greeters, former Iowa governor Robert Ray, his wife, Billie, and local philanthropist Maddie Levitt. Unfortunately, the 1886 building lacked insulation, was not air conditioned, and because of an oversight, its windows, which had been nailed shut for the winter, remained sealed and could not be opened. It was stifling inside, but the evening was still a great success. Governor Ray was amazed at the turnout, telling Susan Terry that "all of [Des Moines] society was here." Besides paying the $25 admission, attendees bid generously on the twenty live auction packages and forty-three items in the silent auction, and the Blue Ribbon Foundation raised over $100,000.[8]

This success ensured that the Corndog Kickoff became an annual event. Its format has remained largely unchanged, but it has grown substantially. Two thousand people attended the 2016 benefit, raising a record $685,000 for fair restoration. All told, the twenty Corndog Kickoff parties have netted the foundation $4.7 million.[9]

As discussions for the first Corndog Kickoff went forward, Putney ran into some problems with the way work had been divided between the fair itself and the foundation. While Putney handled fund-raising, Kathie Swift, the fair's marketing manager, sold annual sponsorships for attractions and events at the fair, but neither she nor Putney kept close track of what the other was doing. Putney had encountered some issues early on when asking for donations only to learn that the entities solicited had already been tapped for a sponsorship at the fair. The last straw for him came when he and Governor Terry Branstad met with Lynn Horak, CEO of Norwest Bank (now Wells Fargo), and asked for a gift of $500,000. Horak turned them down, and Putney soon discovered that the fair had sold Norwest a sponsorship for the fairground's Family Center for $10,000. The bank's name was prominently displayed on the building. "Why," Putney recalled, "would you give a half million when $10,000 got you all the visibility you wanted?"[10]

To end this predicament, he went to the Fair Board and Marion Lucas, explaining that sponsorships should be placed under his control so they could be coordinated with the foundation's gift requests. He also thought he could link the two, tying large donations and sponsorships together. Putney's appeal raised concerns among some board members and fair staff who saw it as a power grab, but ultimately Lucas agreed, and the selling of sponsorships was moved to the foundation in 1997. Reinig initially oversaw sponsorships sales.[11]

After the foundation took over, it went after corporate sponsorships more aggressively, and the results were soon visible on the fairgrounds. By 2001, the *Des Moines Register* observed, "Iowans can now gulp the fair's official beer (Miller), drive the fair's official vehicle (Dodge), and lick the fair's official ice cream (Anderson Erickson Dairy)." Other noticeable changes saw the old Fairview Stage renamed Anderson Erickson Dairy Stage, sponsored by KCCI Channel 8 News, and the John Deere Agriculture Building, sponsored by Alliant Energy. And sponsorships brought in large amounts of money. In 2000, for example, sponsorship sales provided $654,000, an increase of 20 percent over the previous year. The funds all went to fair operations, with $400,000 being used that year to pay for free entertainment.[12]

Not long after the foundation took over sponsorships, however, there were staffing changes at the Blue Ribbon Foundation. Reinig had gotten married, and shortly after the 1997 fair, she and her husband moved to Nebraska. It was a real loss for Putney, who had great respect for Reinig and all she had done to help get the foundation off the ground. Emily Reis, who had recently been hired as the foundation's communications director, became Putney's assistant. Soon a separate sponsorship position was created, initially filled by Pam Brocker. Putney's full-time team would remain at three, but the positions were often first jobs for people, and turnover was frequent. Reis left for another job shortly before the fair in 1999, and Amy Houston (now Miller), who started at the foundation as a special programs manager that spring, stepped in to fill the void as the assistant director.[13]

Going forward, Putney continued to rely on young people for much of the foundation's work. Important over the years were Robin Lage (now Taylor), Estee Walter (now Nenow), Kristen Guiter, Jennifer Carver (now Cannon), Bridget Blair (now Anderson), Emily Barnd (now Saveraid), and Allyson Dierenfeld (now Krull), who either handled sponsorships or special programs, or managed communications. All brought high energy, enthusiasm, and fresh ideas, but retention remained a problem, and all but one left for other jobs after a few years. The exception was Robin Lage, who joined the foundation in 1999 to manage special programs.[14]

Three years later, in 2002, Lage became the foundation's assistant director when Amy Houston resigned to finish law school. Like her predecessors, Lage ultimately became a jack-of-all-trades, overseeing the Blue Ribbon Foundation's merchandise, volunteer and planned giving programs, writing grants, maintaining the foundation's books, and organizing the auction for the Corndog Kickoff. But unlike Reinig or Houston, she made the job a career and remains in this position today. Lage explained her longevity: "To know you are involved in creating happiness and competition at the fair that is inherently good and fun and traditional…is so fulfilling. Where else can you get that?"[15]

Meanwhile, just before Reinig left, the foundation introduced the "Iowan of the Day" program at the 1997 fair. It was designed to recognize citizens who through volunteer work, community activity, or philanthropic efforts made Iowa a better place to live. Each year a panel of judges would pick ten winners from nominations, and during each of the first ten days of the fair, one of these individuals was honored at a ceremony on the Bill Riley Stage. Winners would receive a cash prize, four admission tickets to the fair, special parking, four tickets to the Grandstand show, use of a golf cart during the fair, a one-night stay at the downtown Des Moines Marriott Hotel, and a one-year subscription to *The Iowan* magazine.[16]

Putney got Duane "Speed" Herrig, the owner of Cookies Food Products, a barbeque sauce company, to sponsor the award. Herrig first noted how run down the fair's facilities were in 1988, when he was working the World Pork Expo at the fairgrounds and saw bricks on the ground that had crumbled and fallen off the Grandstand. He recalled, "It was disappointing to see the great Iowa State Fair in that kind of shape." So Herrig was primed and ready to help when he met Putney several years later. His assistance began in 1996, when he and his crew provided the food for the foundation's annual appreciation golf outing and continued to do so over the thirteen years the event was held. Cookies Food Products remains the major underwriter of "Iowan of the Day" today.[17]

Once partnered with Herrig, Putney was happy to celebrate Iowans with the award, but he also envisioned the program as a way to make connections with community leaders from around the state. Relationships begun with some of these individuals might result in support for the fair.[18]

Among the first group selected for "Iowan of the Day" was wealthy businessman Bill Knapp. The recognition was well deserved. Besides making a big splash earlier that year with his $1 million donation to the fair, Knapp had built Iowa Realty into the dominant real estate company in the state. He was a key figure in downtown Des Moines's resurgence in the 1980s and 1990s, led the revival of the deteriorating Drake University neighborhood, and had become one of the city's foremost philanthropists. Knapp and companion Susan Terry had camped at the fair that summer, squeezed into a spot Putney had found for them at the campground. They enjoyed it so much that Terry called Putney in the fall asking if she and Knapp could camp at the fair the following year as well. Putney was thrilled they were planning to return, but then Terry threw him a curve when she said they were interested in a campsite "upgrade." He asked what she was thinking, and Terry responded that she and Knapp wanted to locate east of the Livestock Pavilion and kitty-corner from where he and Emily had established the Blue Ribbon compound. "Shoot," Putney replied, "I don't know if I can make that happen."[19]

He knew the request would raise eyebrows among some Fair Board members and others concerned about the inequity of one couple being given such an unprecedented camping spot, but for Putney, the move was critical. He understood that keeping Knapp happy and excited about the fair was important because many influential and wealthy people followed Knapp's lead. Putney ultimately convinced Lucas that letting Knapp and Terry set up their luxury trailer on the prime fairgrounds real estate just up the path from the Putneys' campsite was wise, and starting in 1998, this became the couple's home base during the fair's eleven days in August.[20]

Jerry Parkin, Deere & Company's state government affairs director and soon a member of the Fair Board, recalled: "Knapp was instrumental in moving the fund-raising forward. His contribution was different than Pioneer's or Deere's because he was an individual Iowan making a huge commitment to the fair. The camping spot cemented it. From there, he made others see the value of supporting the fair." Indeed, Knapp and Terry, who would be married that fall, increased the number of gatherings they held at their campsite, hosting catered cocktail parties and dinners almost every night of the fair for their friends. The list of those passing through the Knapp campsite looked like a page of Who's Who in Des Moines and included the Elwells, the Cownies, the Kenyons, and the Horners, all of whom became significant donors to the Blue Ribbon Foundation.[21]

In 2004, the Knapps and the Putneys improved their campsites. The Knapps' site was leveled and landscaped, a concrete slab was poured, and a retaining wall was constructed. For the duration of the fair, a large party tent was put up, a trailer equipped for the caterers was brought in, and the Knapps soon swapped their upscale trailer for a luxury motor coach. Clearly happy with his fair accommodations, Knapp explained to a *Des Moines Register* reporter, "It's pretty nice when your house goes with you."[22]

As Putney expected, Knapp's impact was almost immediate. Shortly after the announcement of the businessman's large gift, the Fair Board began moving forward with their ideas for updating the Varied Industries Building. By fall 1998 the board had settled on a design by the Des Moines architectural firm of Kendall Griffith Russell Artiaga. Plans called for preserving the building's main entrance to the north as well as the northwest and northeast porticos and then demolishing the rest, replacing it with a massive enclosed column-free pavilion as well as two stories of breakout rooms in an eastern wing.[23]

There were problems, however, aligning this proposal with the Fair Board's budget. Eventually Lucas and the board decided to scrap these plans altogether and start over, going with a design by Keffer/Overton Associates, a descendant of the architectural firm that had built the original structure in 1911. Their scheme called for enclosing and renovating the open-air structure while removing 25 percent of the interior columns to create more flexible exhibit space, replacing the roof and floor, and installing heating and cooling, which would make the huge two-acre hall available for year-round use. A 43,000-square-foot addition with meeting rooms, offices, storage, and restrooms would extend the structure to the south.[24]

As this planning moved forward, Putney lobbied the legislature for $10 million for the building renovation. He adeptly used the Knapp gift to push legislators for the funds, emphasizing that an individual Iowan had given $1 million toward the project, and now it was the state's turn to contribute to the betterment of the state-owned fairgrounds. Knapp, meanwhile, one of the state's most influential Democrats, made some calls, coaxing those at the statehouse to support the funding measure.[25]

The effort worked. Governor Tom Vilsack signed the bill in spring 1999, providing $10 million for work on the Varied Industries Building, which would be completed in phases over two years, with the remodeling of the existing structure followed by the addition. A groundbreaking ceremony took place on the last day of the 2000 Iowa State Fair. But as construction got underway, the project hit a potential snag. That October, it was reported that architects at Keffer/Overton had not submitted plans for the building to state historical officials before the work was done, which was required by Iowa law because the fairgrounds was listed on the National Register of Historic Places. Ralph Christian, architectural historian for the State Historical Society of Iowa, noted that no plans were submitted for the building addition. "There could be a problem with it," he explained. "We don't know." If the work largely altered the historical integrity of the original architecture, state officials had the authority to vote the fairgrounds off the National Register.[26]

Judy McClure, historic preservation architect for the State Historical Society, was not nearly as concerned as Christian and thought the changes would probably be tolerable, saying, "It would have to be something pretty horrendous before we'd rattle the cage." Keffer/Overton architect Scott Worth was caught off guard by the concerns. He had not submitted the plans to state officials because the firm did not believe the project affected the building's historical significance, but he promised to consult with them from that point forward. Ultimately the controversy died down, and in December the *Register* editorialized, "In short, the Varied Industries Building will look better than it has in years, and it will be functional year-round." But the editorial did call for greater collaboration: "The State Fair Board should run the second phase of the project and future fairgrounds projects past state historical officials. They can't veto plans, but they can offer valuable expertise on modernizing historically significant buildings."[27]

Renovation of the original structure was completed by the summer of 2001. Now named the William C. Knapp Varied Industries Building, it was dedicated on August 9, the day before that year's fair began. Knapp used a giant pair of scissors for the ribbon cutting in a ceremony attended by Governor Tom Vilsack, Speaker of the Iowa House Brent Siegrist, and other state representatives and dignitaries, as well as Putney and Fair Board members and staff. At the fair's end, manager Marion Lucas noted that the remodeled, air-conditioned exhibition hall was one of the summer extravaganza's biggest hits. The following year, much to the delight of attendees, the Corndog Kickoff was moved from the Agriculture Building, which had replaced Pioneer Hall as the event's venue, to the fully climate-controlled Varied Industries Building, "So," the foundation's Blue Ribbon newsletter explained, "when corndogs sizzle and auction bidding gets hot, you'll stay cool."[28]

Longtime Fair Board member Don Greiman saw the transformation of the Varied Industries Building as a major turning point for the fair because it opened the door to a significant off-season business. In February and March 2002, for instance, the building hosted a sports show, a classic car auction, and a flower, lawn, and garden show. Many more such programs followed, and Greiman believed these frequently attracted people who had never been to the fairgrounds before, often leading them to attend other events at the site, including the State Fair. Architect Scott Worth agreed, calling the newly enclosed structure "the springboard" for what the fair is today.[29]

By the time the addition to the Varied Industries Building was completed, the Blue Ribbon Foundation had raised $50 million for the restoration and preservation of the fairgrounds. Its success made more upgrades possible, including the Hy-Vee Fun Forest, a $400,000 landscaping project behind the Agriculture Building and next to Pella Plaza, and a new roof on the Cattle Barn, which also got new offices, restrooms, and showers. Then horse racing, or at least gambling, finally came in for the fair. Years earlier, pari-mutuel betting at the fairgrounds had failed to produce the windfall backers expected. The effort was clearly hurt by the opening of Prairie Meadows Race Track in Altoona, a suburb northeast of the fairgrounds, in 1989. The horse track could not survive alone, however, and in 1995, Prairie Meadows added casino gambling to its operation. After that, it began generating a lot of revenue for Polk County and the state of Iowa through taxes and grants. In 2001, the Blue Ribbon Foundation received an $800,000 grant from Prairie Meadows designated for a new roof for the Livestock Pavilion.[30]

In addition to replacing the huge, three-tiered roof, the Livestock Pavilion received further updating when a gift from Fair Board member Bob Schlutz and his wife, Marillyn, funded a heating and air-conditioning system. Now climate-controlled, the pavilion became a much more comfortable venue for livestock shows.[31]

When this renovation was completed, most of the fair's major facilities had been restored. The Register explained the feat: "While new roofs and brick-and-mortar replacement on barns and exhibit halls built in the 19th century and early 20th may seem a modest achievement, they are critically important to preserving the essence of what the fair means to Iowa....The State Fair is the most visible link between past and present, urban and rural, a showcase for the best of all facets of Iowa's economy." Scott Worth, the Keffer/Overton architect who oversaw the work on the Varied Industries Building, agreed that the graceful, historic buildings were integral to the Iowa State Fair and that saving them was critical because as he put it, "You can't build history."[32]

Meanwhile, Putney had been thinking about developing a book to chronicle the Iowa State Fair. Although the fair had spawned the well-known Phil Stong novel and then film and stage versions of the story, no popular history of the Iowa institution had been written. He now moved to remedy this. First he contacted local author Mary Kay Shanley, who among other things had written a book about his sister-in-law called *She Taught Me How to Eat Artichokes*. When Shanley expressed interest, Putney went to Maddie Levitt, who agreed to underwrite the effort. The project got underway in 1999. New young staffer Amy Houston did the research and oversaw the endeavor while Shanley wrote the text and artist Paul Micich designed it. The lavish coffee-table volume, entitled *Our State Fair: Iowa's Blue Ribbon Story*, was published in 2000 and celebrated the fair and its history. Chock-full of photographs and illustrations, it included a lively narrative examining the fair's history, agricultural competitions and exhibits, entertainments, and the buildings and grounds. The book did exactly what Putney had hoped: it provided a new means of getting the fair's story out to a broad audience and gave the foundation another popular item to sell.[33]

As research for the book project began, Putney became aware of the inadequacy of the fair museum, which had been opened in 1982 and was housed in the Polk County Building on the grounds northeast of Pioneer Hall. The wooden structure dated back to 1887, originally erected as a place for residents of the Polk County Poor Farm to relax and eat while visiting the fair. Seven years after the poor farm closed in 1972, the building was turned over to the Fair Board, and three years later, it opened as the museum. Unfortunately, Putney learned that a lot of pertinent, historic fair material was not there but held in the archives of the State Historical Building in downtown Des Moines. Likewise, he worried that the artifacts and documents held in the fairground's old building were not secure and needed a sturdy, climate-controlled facility.[34]

These realities prompted Putney to acquire copies of fair documents held at the State Historical Building so they could be included onsite with other fair material. It also led the foundation's executive director and the Fair Board to consider a new fair museum. The idea soon transformed into a bigger project calling for refurbishing the old museum while adding a new facility. Besides exhibiting fair artifacts and memorabilia, the new complex would offer a secure place to store valuable artifacts and a modern interactive display providing fairgoers the story of key moments in fair history. When Putney began looking for potential donors for the museum complex, he first spoke with Helen Deets, wife of Floyd Deets, the former superintendent of buildings and grounds at the Iowa State Fair who had initially headed up the State Fair museum. She suggested that her nephew, Des Moines businessman Richard (Dick) Easter, might be interested in helping. Putney pitched the idea to him, and Easter pledged $300,000 to the project.[35]

During Putney's search for donors for the complex, the Des Moines Register ran an investigative piece about the Blue Ribbon Foundation in August 2003, shortly before that year's fair began. Reporters Bert Dalmer and Ken Fuson acknowledged the foundation's achievements in fund-raising, bringing in nearly $54 million for restoring the iconic fairgrounds, but they also noted that the state of Iowa was the biggest contributor, besting private donors by a two-to-one margin. This was the exact opposite of what a consultant had proposed when the foundation was created in 1991. Clearly Putney and the foundation had aggressively gone after state appropriations and had succeeded in getting big money—$36 million—where previous fair efforts had largely failed. To Putney's mind, this was perfectly fitting because the Iowa State Fair and the fairgrounds were owned by the state of Iowa. He was proud of his work with the foundation and explained to the reporters, "If the original plan was to raise $2 in private donations for every $1 in state appropriations, nobody told me."[36]

Others involved with the fair had nothing but praise for Putney and his leadership of the foundation. Back in 1991, Governor Branstad had suggested that the Blue Ribbon's efforts might be modeled after the fund-raising campaign for the State Historical Building in the 1980s, where private donors shouldered two-thirds of the cost. Even though that had not happened, he was thrilled with the amounts raised by the foundation, which exceeded all his expectations. Bill Riley, who along with David Oman had headed the foundation on a voluntary basis as it struggled during its first year of operation, said Putney "really turned it around." Bill Knapp was blunter: "I don't know where the fair would be if it wasn't for him." Before his efforts at the foundation, Knapp noted, "The state absolutely let this fair go to where it was a mess."[37]

But the exposé had a surprising, unintended consequence. The afternoon the story ran, Putney received a call from Richard (Dick) Jacobson, a wealthy Des Moines philanthropist who had made his money in the warehouse and trucking business. Putney had been building a relationship with Jacobson and had asked him for $300,000 for the museum project. Jacobson did not commit initially, but after reading the *Register* story and what he interpreted as its accusatory tone, he pledged the entire amount. A flabbergasted Putney gladly accepted.[38]

The groundbreaking ceremony for the new museum took place during the August 2003 fair, with the building scheduled to be ready for the Iowa State Fair's 2004 sesquicentennial. Putney found two other large donors interested in supporting the museum over the next couple of years. First was Des Moines businessman Ron Kenyon, who had been successful in the construction and paving business. Bill and Susan Knapp had invited Kenyon and his wife, Margaret, to their fair campsite for dinner one evening in 2004 and asked John and Emily Putney to join them. This meeting led to Putney visiting with the Kenyons over lunch at the Des Moines Club, where he explained the planned interactive displays for the new museum. The Kenyons were enthused and asked about the cost. Putney told them $400,000, but the visit ended with nothing else said. Shortly after that, Putney remembered, "Ron called me up and said to come to his office. When I got there, he wrote me a check for $400,000." Later the Kenyon family, through daughter Rhonda Hill and her husband, Derek, gave another $200,000 toward the museum complex. The interactive Ronald and Margaret Kenyon Gallery debuted in the new museum building—the Richard O. Jacobson Hall—at the 2005 fair.[39]

That same year, Putney secured another $300,000 for beginning the restoration of the old museum building from another Deets family member, Sally Smith, and her husband, Chuck, of Atlanta, Georgia. Sally's grandfather, Henry Deets, had been the fair superintendent before his son Floyd took over, and her father, Ralph (Floyd's brother), had been raised on the fairgrounds and worked for fair maintenance. Additional $100,000 gifts from Dick and Sherry Easter, Maddie Levitt, and Rod and Connie French made the completion of the facility possible, and the Ralph H. Deets Historical Museum was dedicated during the 2007 fair. It had been fully refurbished and included a new basement and addition with an elevator, storage, and exhibit rooms. This building, along with Jacobson Hall, made up the new Richard L. Easter Museum Complex.[40]

Several important changes took place while the museum improvements moved from drawing board to reality. First, fair manager Marion Lucas chose to take early retirement in 2001. During his fifteen-year tenure, fair attendance rose from 732,000 to 939,000 and its budget more than tripled. These accomplishments were clearly made possible because Lucas and the Fair Board had the foresight to create the Blue Ribbon Foundation, which had turned the fair's fortunes around. Dave Huinker, then president of the Fair Board, had nothing but praise for Lucas: "What he's done is immeasurable. He put the Iowa State Fair on the map with the livestock shows and the renovation work. The fairgrounds has really become a showplace." So much so, in fact, that officials from other fairs began visiting the Iowa State Fair, seeking the reasons for its success. Many concluded that they needed fund-raising entities similar to the Blue Ribbon Foundation, and imitations began popping up.[41]

Regionally, foundations were established at the Missouri State Fair in 1998, the Minnesota State Fair in 2002, the Kansas State Fair in 2003, the Illinois State Fair in 2006, and the Indiana State Fair in 2011. Some of these organizations borrowed liberally from the Blue Ribbon Foundation's playbook. Representatives from the Kansas State Fair, for instance, visited the Corndog Kickoff in 2006 hoping to "steal ideas," while the Illinois organization created its own "Corndog Kickoff" and an "Illinoisian of the Day" program.[42]

The Iowa State Fair's prominence was certainly a major reason why Gary Slater, a former staffer at the exhibition, was interested in returning as manager. Slater grew up on a farm in Missouri, and shortly after graduating from the University of Missouri in 1981, he got into the fair business, starting as a livestock supervisor at the Missouri State Fair. Here he had worked under Marion Lucas. After Lucas moved to manage the Iowa State Fair in 1986, he hired Slater the following year to oversee sponsorships, but the job soon expanded to managing free entertainment and off-season events as well. Slater remained there five years before leaving to work for the National Pork Producers Council as manager of its World Pork Expo. Six years later, he returned to the fair business, becoming director of the Missouri State Fair from 1997 to 2001. That April, he was hired as the manager of the Iowa State Fair and became manager and CEO when Lucas stepped down the following January.[43]

Shortly after Slater took over, he and Putney began discussing relocating the foundation office, which had been in downtown Des Moines since its inception so Putney could network easily with the city's rich and powerful. Originally headquartered on the ninth floor of Two Ruan Center, the office had moved to a larger space on the seventeenth floor of the adjacent Ruan Center in February 2000. But by 2002, Putney was plugged into the Des Moines community, and remaining downtown became less important. At the same time, space on the fairgrounds opened up when Lucas retired, and he and his wife, Fran, moved out of the Earth Home, where they had lived over the past few years. Both Slater and Putney agreed that having the foundation on the grounds with the rest of the fair's administrators now made sense, and since Slater and his family had taken up residence in the traditional manager's house, the Blue Ribbon staff moved into the Earth Home that June.[44]

There was one more major change that year; John Putney was elected to the Iowa State Senate. He had never considered such service until his years of lobbying for the fair at the Iowa Statehouse had acquainted him with many legislators and familiarized him with current political issues. This combined with a recent reapportionment of Benton, Grundy, and Tama Counties, which reconfigured the district where Putney lived to the same way it had been in the 1950s when his father, Lawrence, had served in Iowa's house and senate. Putney knew a lot of people in the district, and after talking with his wife, Emily, as well as Lucas, Slater, and the Fair Board, he decided to throw his hat into the ring and won.[45]

Putney had to give up lobbying for the fair, a role that was taken over by lobbyist Brian Johnson, and knew "he had to tow a fine line with respect to conflicts regarding issues and appropriations associated with the fair." He also had less time to devote to his work at the foundation. Still, he felt certain his "service in the senate was valuable to the fair just as a teacher [in the legislature] looks out for education issues or a farmer for agricultural issues." So too could he address matters affecting the Iowa State Fair.[46]

Despite Putney's work in the senate, which included leadership roles such as Republican Party whip, the Blue Ribbon Foundation did not miss a beat—more money was raised and more fair upgrades were funded. Continuity remained the story.

In 2002, the Fair Board went forward with its plans for Legacy Terrace, which would replace a concrete stage on the Grand Concourse in front of the Grandstand. "The thought," Robin Lage, the foundation's assistant director, explained, "was to add green space, to bring back the park-like feeling of the fairgrounds." The project got started with contributions in memory of Bill Partlow and Max Bishop, two former State Fair Board members, and Alan Triggs, son of longtime State Fair Board member Merritt Triggs. Initially the terrace included grass and trees, benches and granite pavers, and was opened at the 2002 fair. Over the next couple of years, more trees, benches, and pavers were added, as well as a "dancing waters" fountain, where children could frolic during the hot weather of the fair.[47]

Adept at putting people and projects together, Putney looked to Bob and Sheri Horner to help finance the fountain. The Horners loved the fair, and Bob Horner's Des Moines Asphalt and Paving Company often donated paving services to the fairgrounds. Marion Lucas always gratefully responded to these donations by giving the Horners prime tickets to all the Grandstand shows at the fair. Putney met the Horners through his brother, Mark, and got to know them better at fair events, including parties at the Knapp campsite. Here he became aware of their love of Grandstand shows, and this made him think they would be interested in contributing to this project, which would be located in front of their favorite fair venue. He was right; at his request, the Horners donated $50,000 to underwrite the water feature at the entrance to the terrace.[48]

Meanwhile, Susan Knapp came up with an idea that would make the foundation some money. Several years earlier, Bells, the Knapps' Labrador Retriever, broke free from her leash at the family's campsite and wandered around the Iowa State Fairgrounds for a couple of hours before she was found by livestock control staff. The incident led Susan to write a children's story, *Bells Goes to the Fair*, which she had illustrated by her cousin, John Whitehurst. It was published in 2002 and went on sale at that year's fair. The Knapps paid to produce the book and donated all proceeds from the sales to the Blue Ribbon Foundation. The following year, Iowa First Lady Christie Vilsack selected the book for her literacy program, and she and Susan raised $100,000 to print and distribute it to forty-one thousand kindergarteners across the state. All told, the book generated roughly $65,000 for the foundation.[49]

By mid-decade, the Iowa State Fair was the envy of fair officials across the nation. Slater was pleased, noting that the fair "had really flourished" and was in better shape physically and financially than it had ever been. Attendance topped one million for the first time in 2002, and this feat would be repeated twelve out of the next fourteen years. With the fair now thriving, Slater and the Fair Board began acquiring additional land for expansion. Specifically, they were buying up homes along the southwest portion of the grounds and also thinking of developing a master plan focused on traffic patterns at the fairgrounds. They asked Keffer/Overton, which had overseen most of the fair work since the Grandstand renovation in the late 1990s, to help with a new master plan for the fairgrounds in 2004. A key element of the plan was an east–west pedestrian walkway through the middle of the grounds to relieve congestion on the Grand Concourse and make getting around the fair easier. However, the walkway would remain a dream for ten years before it was realized when the Ruan family made a large donation.[50]

Also mentioned during master plan discussions was the need for repairs on the Swine Barn, which underwent a major renovation in 2005 and 2006, including masonry repair and tuck-pointing, a new roof, and new stalls. While this work was taking place, Slater and Putney began considering new facilities for the fair. Fairgoers had long loved the farrowing display located in the Swine Barn, and Slater thought adding a larger animal birthing exhibit would prove both popular and educational. After visiting such birthing centers at the Minnesota State Fair and Tulsa State Fair, Slater and Putney decided that a similar center should be a top priority in Des Moines. It was also clear that a larger amphitheater for free entertainment was needed.[51]

Meanwhile, Bill Hare, the fair's senior plant operations director who had succeeded Floyd Deets, prepared to retire. Fair Board member Bob Schlutz discussed the position with Slater and suggested that if possible, they hire an architect as plant manager because plans called for a lot of building in the future and having such a person on staff would save time and money. Slater and others agreed. At the same time, Scott Worth was considering opportunities beyond Keffer/Overton. Worth's familiarity with the fair and his work on its facilities since the 1990s made him the ideal candidate, and he was hired to head plant operations in 2005. Almost immediately he was tasked with developing plans for refurbishing the old museum building and a new amphitheater, with both projects commencing after that year's fair. The following year, he designed the animal birthing center.[52]

Funds for the museum's upgrade had already been secured, but when a large gift for the amphitheater, which was underway, fell through, Putney scrambled to make up the contribution. In June 2006, just a couple of months before the stage's completion, Putney hosted the foundation's annual golf appreciation outing. Here he talked to Bill Knapp about the lost donor and the next project on the horizon—the animal birthing center. Without being asked for money, Knapp inquired about the cost of both projects and how much Putney needed. The foundation's director said each structure was about $1.5 million, and he would be very happy with $750,000 for either one. Knapp replied that he might be interested.[53]

The next day he called Putney and asked, "Which project do you think is better?" "They're equal," was the response. "Well," Knapp answered, "then I'll take both of them," giving the foundation $750,000 for each project. The open-air stage replaced the old American Republic stage in the fair's Heritage Village in the northeast portion of the grounds. Named the Susan Knapp Amphitheater in honor of Bill's wife, it was the fair's largest free entertainment venue and could accommodate an audience of five thousand. It debuted at the 2006 fair, which also saw the groundbreaking for the birthing center, christened the Paul R. Knapp Animal Learning Center in honor of Bill's brother. Bill Knapp was enthused about the facility: "We are excited to be involved with such an important addition to the Fairgrounds." To encourage others, he added, "The Iowa State Fair is one of our favorite causes, and as we support enhancement of the buildings and grounds, we hope others will contribute as well."[54]

Appropriately, Bill and Susan Knapp were honored that year by being named grand marshals for the 2007 Iowa State Fair Parade, the annual event that winds through downtown Des Moines and kicks off the summer exhibition. The following morning at the fair's opening day festivities, a ribbon-cutting ceremony was held at the completed Paul R. Knapp Animal Learning Center. The *Register*'s Rox Laird applauded this new structure, explaining that the fair was rightly evolving to reflect "the urbanization of Iowa." As Iowans were becoming further removed from the farm, fair officials "felt it necessary to create a new exhibit that demonstrates where baby animals come from." Here youngsters and their parents could watch farm animals being born and learn about their development. And just as Laird had predicted, the facility became very popular with fairgoers.[55]

Besides giving money, encouraging others to give, and introducing many of his wealthy friends to the fair, Knapp sometimes played a more direct role in fund-raising for the Blue Ribbon Foundation. A couple of years earlier, in 2005, fair officials had identified several buildings on the grounds that needed renovating. Topping the list was the Cultural Center. Putney and Knapp began talking about securing a lead gift for the project and soon had Des Moines businessman Jim Cownie in their sights. Cownie was a good friend of Knapp's and had made a lot of money in the cable industry, co-founding Heritage Communications in the 1970s and eventually selling it to then cable giant Tele-Communications Inc. (TCI) in the late 1980s. One evening during the 2006 fair, Putney, Knapp, and Slater took a golf cart to see Jim and Patty Cownie, who were having a drink at the Bird's Nest, their son Drew's bar and grill at the fairgrounds.[56]

In the midst of the conversation with the Cownies, Knapp decided the time was right to make the pitch, and he asked the couple for $750,000 toward refurbishing the Cultural Center, just east of where they were sitting. They readily agreed, eventually throwing in an additional $250,000 toward the building's overhaul. The structure was immediately renamed the Patty and Jim Cownie Cultural Center in their honor, with the extensive $2.8 million face-lift, which included the additions of air conditioning, elevators, exhibit space, and more restrooms, taking place in three phases from 2012 to 2014.[57]

Knapp played a somewhat similar role in 2007 with wealthy Ankeny entrepreneur Denny Elwell, this time involving a fair project in the very early discussion phase that was bubbling to the top because of donor interest. Putney had been courting Elwell for years. His family had enjoyed the fair for five generations, and Elwell had contributed to a variety of fair programs, such as the Corndog Kickoff. However, Putney believed Elwell wanted to support a larger project if the right one could be found. Indeed, Elwell's parents had recently died, and the businessman was looking for a way to honor them. At the same time, Slater and the Fair Board began considering improvements to the Family Center (now the Maytag Family Theaters next to the Department of Natural Resources Building) because it was becoming too small for the food department's contests and activities, which it had housed since 1982. One idea called for converting the Iowa Tourism Building, slightly southwest of the Knapp Varied Industries Building, into a new, larger food center.[58]

In early spring 2007, Bill Knapp and Denny Elwell had lunch. When the conversation turned to the fair, Knapp told him about the talk of a new food center. He knew Elwell's family had been in the grocery business and thought the idea might pique his interest. Putney thought so as well and had asked Scott Worth for some simple sketches of what the repurposed building might look like. Before long, Elwell contacted Putney, who told him naming rights to convert the building to the food center would be $1 million. He then showed Elwell the preliminary drawings Worth had done. Elwell and his wife, Candy, pledged the full amount that May. The building was renamed the Elwell Family Food Center for the 2007 fair. Food competitions were moved, and the tourism exhibits were relocated to the Varied Industries Building. Following the fair, the cinder block structure was stripped down to its frame, expanded, and then completely rebuilt. The new $2 million climate-controlled facility was larger and much more appealing than the old metal tourism building and provided another new structure available for year-round use. It was finished in time for the 2009 fair.[59]

The same year of the Elwell pledge, the Knapps and the Putneys took a trip together to Columbus, Ohio, where Susan, an accomplished equestrian, was competing in the All-American Quarter Horse Congress. While there, Emily went shopping and came across a silver pendant with a small blue gemstone in the shape of an award ribbon. A blue ribbon, she thought. She bought one and did some research on where they were manufactured. After talking with her husband, she started a very exclusive club, giving female donors or wives of donors who contributed $1 million or more to the foundation one of the special pendants. Susan Knapp, Patty Cownie, and Candy Elwell were the first to receive these exclusive "million-dollar necklaces." Emily Putney continues the tradition to this day.[60]

A couple of months before the trip to Columbus, Putney decided that as his second term in the senate waned, he would not seek a third term the following year. Although the foundation had continued enjoying success during his time in the legislature, he explained, "It was time for me to retire and return full-time, full-bore to the work of the Foundation." The move was clearly influenced by the Fair Board's decision to go forward with an ambitious $20 million capital project, which included building a new agricultural exhibition arena intended to attract national "equine, livestock, and other agriculturally-related shows, exhibitions, and conventions" and adding a multipurpose stalling barn. Because prime sites were at a premium on the fairgrounds, this would require relocating existing fair facilities elsewhere on the grounds. And since the fair had recently acquired additional land, new infrastructure such as roads, parking, and moving an electrical substation were also necessary.[61]

A year earlier, Putney had seen what might serve as a model for the fair's proposed indoor arena. At the end of August 2006, he and his wife, Emily, had accompanied the Knapps on a trip to Texas, where Susan had competed in the American Quarter Horse Association's Bayer Select World Championship at the Amarillo National Center. Putney and Knapp had been especially impressed by the facility, and with an eye to building a similar structure at the Iowa State Fair, they checked "all its nooks and crannies."[62]

They returned to Des Moines excited about what they had seen in Amarillo, and after discussions with Slater and the Fair Board, Putney and Slater put together a group to visit the Amarillo National Center and a similar facility at the Tulsa State Fairgrounds in Oklahoma. In addition to the foundation's executive director and the fair manager, others on the trip included Knapp, Fair Board members Jerry Parkin and Paul Vaassen, architect Scott Worth, and potential donor Bruce Rastetter. Dwayne McAninch—another big fair supporter who over the years had contributed more than $100,000 to the foundation and whose Des Moines-based earthmoving firm, the McAninch Corporation, had provided the grading and site preparation for the Paul R. Knapp Animal Learning Center gratis—went as well, flying the group to Texas and Oklahoma on his private jet in early 2007.[63]

As plans for the project developed, fair officials requested $11 million in state funds for the 2008 fiscal year. Lobbyist Brian Johnson pushed the case, Knapp made some phone calls, and Governor Chet Culver included an $11 million appropriation for the improvements in his 2008 budget, contingent upon the fair raising the rest from private donors. The fair received a first installment of $3 million from the legislature that year and would get the rest over the next two years. Meanwhile, ground for the three-year project had been broken at the 2007 fair. Because of its complexity and, in Worth's words, "all the moving parts," Worth brought in his former colleagues at Keffer/Overton for assistance.[64]

Besides important infrastructure work, phase one of the construction required moving the covered outdoor arena, originally located west of the Horse Barn, to make room for the new agricultural exhibition arena. The outdoor arena and a new multipurpose stalling barn were erected just east of the Swine Barn where the ice and feed building had been. A temporary structure for these was put up, and the following year a permanent ice and feed building was constructed up the hill to the northeast, by the entrance to the campgrounds. While this work was being done for the opening of the 2008 fair, the foundation made two big announcements.[65]

Putney had continued talking with Dick Jacobson after he gave money for the fair's museum complex a decade earlier. Now Jacobson was ready to make a much more significant commitment. That summer he pledged $3.5 million to the fair, its largest gift from a private donor. The funds were directed toward the new arena project, which would be named the Richard O. Jacobson Exhibition Center. At the announcement, Jacobson said, "The Fair is the single biggest attraction in the state of Iowa and has been for over 150 years. Iowa has been good to me, and this is a great opportunity to give back to the people of Iowa. I am pleased to be part of this exciting project."[66]

That same August day, the foundation announced another big gift. While Putney was discussing the proposed arena with Jacobson, he was also talking with Bruce Rastetter, one of Jacobson's good friends. A successful entrepreneur from Alden, a small town seventy-five miles north of Des Moines, Rastetter's companies included ethanol producer Hawkeye Renewables and Summit Farms, an agribusiness that produced row crops, beef, swine, and draft horses. He had been a longtime exhibitor of draft horses at the fair and a major supporter of the Sale of Champions. Putney had become acquainted with him years earlier through the cattle business and Republican politics. By 2007, Putney considered Rastetter a potential donor for the planned exhibition center and invited him to join the fair group visiting the arenas in Amarillo and Tulsa. During the trip, Knapp pulled Rastetter aside and explained that the fair needed $1 million from him for the arena. He did not commit, but Knapp had planted the seed. Putney continued cultivating the relationship and pursing the donation, and that summer of 2008, Rastetter pledged $1 million toward the project. In honor of the gift, the fair's 4-H Building was renamed the Bruce L. Rastetter 4-H Exhibits Building.[67]

Phases two and three commenced after the 2008 fair and consisted largely of erecting the Jacobson Center. Scott Worth took a number of design cues from the Amarillo and Tulsa facilities, which were "great arenas for horse shows and competitions," according to Susan Knapp. But Worth noted that both were "big black boxes, relying entirely on artificial light," something he wanted to avoid with the fair's arena. Completed for the 2010 fair, the graceful redbrick center was attached to the Horse Barn to the east by a covered warm-up arena. Inside, it featured a show arena, with skylights spanning the length of the roof providing natural light by day for up to 3,500 spectators. The building also included a balcony overlooking the arena, where, after paying an enrollment fee and yearly dues, members of Jake's Club could enjoy events in the arena from special seating with access to a full bar and food.[68]

Often referred to as "the fair's crown jewel," the Jacobson Center is certainly one of its most important structures. Former board member Don Greiman saw the center as a selling point for the fair and applauded Worth's work on this and other structures on the grounds, noting that he "has such a sense of design and style that the old existing buildings and the new blend." Much as fair officials had expected, the center immediately began attracting big events the fair would not have otherwise gotten. In fact, even before the building was begun, the planned arena had such good buzz in the horse community that the World Percheron Congress scheduled its international show, which featured beautiful draft horses, for the Jacobson Center in October 2010.[69]

The same year the Jacobson Center opened, fairgoers could enjoy a Fair Square, a new treat that also debuted in 2010. The idea for the crispy rice cereal dessert-on-a-stick in either marshmallow or peanut butter flavor grew out of a trip Slater and Putney took to the Washington State Fair in 2009. There they were impressed with Fisher Scones, a staple at that fair for nearly one hundred years. Once back in Des Moines, they asked their staffs to develop a signature dessert for the Iowa State Fair, and the Fair Square was born. The four-ounce bars sold for $2 apiece and gave the Blue Ribbon Foundation a new item to peddle. Over twenty-one thousand Fair Squares were sold that first year, and the gooey delights have remained popular ever since.[70]

At about the same time, several wealthy donors had begun enjoying the fair from their luxury motor homes parked on prime fairgrounds real estate. While the narrow strip of land just up the hill to the east of where the Knapps camped had been home to a few fair superintendents during the exhibition, in recent years the Blue Ribbon Foundation had been auctioning off a campsite there at each Corndog Kickoff. Eventually Denny Elwell asked if he could camp up above the Knapps as well. Putney and Slater agreed, doing everything possible to accommodate the generous benefactor. Soon other $1 million-plus contributors made similar inquiries, and over the next couple of years, Elwell's new neighbors at the fair included Jim and Patty Cownie and Bruce Rastetter. Moe Sinclair, another major fair supporter and owner of a number of Panera Bread franchises in the Midwest, initially camped there as well, though he ceded his spot to MidAmerican Energy in 2014, after the firm donated $1.5 million to the foundation. Today these four campsites are graced with upscale double-wide modular structures that have replaced the motor coaches and are owned by the Iowa State Fair.[71]

As the second decade of the new century opened, it was clear that the foundation had succeeded; the historic fairgrounds had been preserved, and a number of gleaming new buildings added to its appeal. Indeed, the fairgrounds looked better than ever before. With the foundation leading the way, a true renaissance at the Iowa State Fair had taken place. Putney, Slater, and the Fair Board now thought it a good time for a slight change in course. Rather than only raising money and employing it all for immediate upgrades and projects, the foundation also decided to establish an endowment fund "designed to ensure perpetual maintenance and improvement" of the fairgrounds as well as providing another giving option to donors. Rox Laird of the *Register* had suggested such a move as early as 2003: "Now the focus should be on preserving what has been achieved. The State Fair should devote a major share of fund-raising efforts to creating a permanent endowment to provide a continuing source of income for the routine maintenance that had been neglected for so many years. Iowa should never let the fair get in such a condition again."[72]

Creating the fund required a change in Iowa code. Putney and lobbyist Johnson successfully pushed for such a revision, and in spring 2011 Governor Branstad signed the bill allowing the Blue Ribbon Foundation to launch an endowment fund—fittingly named Our Fair's Future. Although it was often more difficult to raise money for an endowment than for capital projects, the fair and foundation believed that when it was funded, the new instrument would act as an insurance policy, guaranteeing in the words of Putney, "a bright future for the Iowa State Fair and its infrastructure." The endowment would also spare the need for another herculean effort to save the fairgrounds.[73]

And there was another major change brewing: Putney was considering retirement. It would not be immediate. Several years earlier, in 2007, he had told Slater that he planned to step down in 2013, after twenty years at the foundation, and he and Slater had worked out a six-year contract. Putney's achievements at the foundation had indeed ushered in a second golden age for the fair; its fortunes had been restored, its facilities renewed and improved, and its beautiful landscaped grounds had been cleaned up and extended. He still had several years left at the fair and several projects he wanted to complete, but as his retirement loomed, many wondered about the foundation's future.[74]

First Blue Ribbon Foundation compound, just east of the Livestock Pavilion during the fair, 1993. Courtesy of the Iowa State Fair Blue Ribbon Foundation.

The upgraded Blue Ribbon Foundation compound, 2012. Courtesy of the Iowa State Fair Blue Ribbon Foundation.

First Corndog Kickoff committee, 1997. From left to right are Lana Jones Gould, Meredith Watters, Suzie Jones, Linda Ruble, Dixie Rhiner, Allison Fleming, Sharon Granzow, Rosalie Gallagher, Susan Terry (Knapp), Joyce Lock, event co-chair, and Dee Wittmack, event co-chair. Courtesy of the Iowa State Fair Blue Ribbon Foundation.

Corndog Kickoff Benefit Auction and Fair Food Grazing Party, Agriculture Building, 2001. Courtesy of the Iowa State Fair Blue Ribbon Foundation.

Jerry Parkin, who joined the Fair Board in 2000, Emily Putney, and
other volunteers selling water at the Blue Ribbon Foundation's water
stand, 1998. Courtesy of the Iowa State Fair Blue Ribbon Foundation.

Bill Knapp speaking at the dedication of the William C. Knapp Varied Industries Building, 2001. Behind Knapp from left to right are Governor Tom Vilsack, John Putney, board member Don Greiman, and Speaker of the Iowa House Brent Siegrest. Courtesy of the Iowa State Fair Blue Ribbon Foundation.

The Earth Home on the fairgrounds has served as the office for the Blue Ribbon Foundation since 2002. Courtesy of the Iowa State Fair Blue Ribbon Foundation.

Dedication ceremony of the Richard L. Easter Museum Complex and Jacobson Hall.
At the blue ribbon from left to right are major project contributors Dwayne McAninch,
Sherry Easter, Richard (Dick) Jacobson, Richard Easter, and Fair Board president C.W.
Thomas, 2004. Courtesy of the Iowa State Fair Blue Ribbon Foundation.

Susan Knapp reading her book, *Bells Goes to the Fair* at the new Susan Knapp
Amphitheater, 2006. Courtesy of the Iowa State Fair Blue Ribbon Foundation.

Crowd enjoying free entertainment at the Susan Knapp Amphitheater, 2008.
Courtesy of the Iowa State Fair Blue Ribbon Foundation.

Patty and Jim Cownie Cultural Center, 2007. Courtesy of the Iowa State
Fair Blue Ribbon Foundation.

Paul R. Knapp Animal Learning Center, 2007. Courtesy of the Iowa State Fair Blue Ribbon Foundation.

Iowa State Fairgrounds, looking east. The MidAmerican Wind Turbine in the upper left is located where Exposition Hall originally stood. In the foreground left to right are the Livestock Pavilion, the Giant Slide, and the Cattle Barn, 2008. Courtesy of the Iowa State Fair Blue Ribbon Foundation.

John Putney, middle, visiting with major donors from left to right Dick Jacobson, Bill Knapp, Bruce Rastetter, and Denny Elwell, 2008. Courtesy of the Iowa State Fair Blue Ribbon Foundation.

Richard O. Jacobson Exhibition Center, 2010. Courtesy of the Iowa State Fair Blue Ribbon Foundation.

John Putney in his golf cart during the 2011 fair. Courtesy of the Iowa State Fair Blue Ribbon Foundation.

Rox Laird, the retired *Des Moines Register* journalist who called for saving the dilapidated Iowa State Fairgrounds and promoted the work of the Blue Ribbon Foundation. Courtesy of Rox Laird.

Robin Taylor, assistant director of the Blue Ribbon Foundation, 2011.
Courtesy of the Iowa State Fair Blue Ribbon Foundation.

Gary Slater, manager and CEO of the Iowa State Fair, 2011. Courtesy of the
Iowa State Fair Blue Ribbon Foundation.

Emily Friedricks, a Blue Ribbon Foundation intern, congratulates Cecil
Rueter on being named Iowan of the Day in 2014. For years, Rueter opened
his golf course near Grand Junction to the foundation for its annual golf
outing. Courtesy of the Iowa State Fair Blue Ribbon Foundation.

Bill Knapp and Jim Cownie in front of "God Bless America," Seward
Johnson's twenty-five-foot American Gothic statue. The two were
responsible for bringing it to the Iowa State Fair in 2014. Courtesy of the
Iowa State Fair Blue Ribbon Foundation.

Peter Cownie, left, and Duane "Speed" Herrig, far right, with Janis and
John Ruan, after the couple received the Iowan of the Day award, 2015.
Courtesy of the Iowa State Fair Blue Ribbon Foundation.

Artist rendering of Ruan Plaza. Its initial phase opened for the 2015 fair.
Courtesy of the Iowa State Fair Blue Ribbon Foundation.

MidAmerican Energy Stage, 2015. Courtesy of the Iowa State
Fair Blue Ribbon Foundation.

The Blue Ribbon
Foundation's "million
dollar necklace." Courtesy
of Susan Knapp.

The Fair Board surprised retiring Blue Ribbon Foundation executive director John Putney at the fair's opening ceremony by naming the Cattle Barn in honor of him and his family, 2013. At the podium is Fair Board president Gary McConnell, while other fair officials, board members, and Lt. Governor Kim Reynolds applaud. Courtesy of the Iowa State Fair Blue Ribbon Foundation.

Peter Cownie, executive director of the Blue Ribbon Foundation, at the 2015 fair's opening ceremony. Courtesy of the Iowa State Fair Blue Ribbon Foundation.

BIGGER AND BETTER

In 2012, a *Des Moines Register* editorial happily crowed, "The Iowa State Fair is one of the nation's largest and oldest expositions of its kind, drawing a million visitors over [its] eleven days [every year]. They come together from across the state to celebrate the state agricultural heritage, industries, arts, culture, and people. The showcase is the historic fairgrounds and buildings that have drawn people to Des Moines for a century and a quarter." The paper also noted that fairgoers would not see "any major new buildings" at that year's fair. "After two decades that have seen the renovation of nearly every building on the grounds and several new ones," it explained, "the fair is taking a breather. But the vision of a fairgrounds for the generations to come is not complete."[1]

If significant building at the fair paused momentarily, John Putney did not. Busy as ever, he continued building relationships, cultivating contributors, and aligning projects with donor interest. He would do so until he announced his retirement in 2013. The millions of dollars he and the foundation had raised had provided for the complete rebuilding of the fair, and its future looked bigger and better than ever when he handed leadership of the foundation over to his successor.

One of the few "brick-and-mortar changes" the *Register* noted at the 2012 fair was the completion of a two-year landscaping project featuring an array of sustainable energy technologies just north of the Cultural Center on Expo Hill, so named because Exposition Hall, one of the fairground's original structures, had graced the rise from 1886 until it was torn down in 1950. The work comprised new walking paths illuminated with LED lighting, solar-powered cooled benches, and solar-powered Wi-Fi benches. Other environmentally oriented elements included permeable pavers and bioswales using native vegetation to eliminate silt and pollution from runoff. A new covered entertainment stage, "shaped by what looks to be a fully inflated sail" in the words of the *Register*, topped off the transformation.[2]

The changes on Expo Hill were made possible through a $250,000 grant the Blue Ribbon Foundation received in 2010, providing federal dollars through state energy agencies, in this case Iowa's Office of Energy Independence, to showcase renewable energy technologies. MidAmerican Energy, which made Putney aware of the grant, agreed to provide the required match of $250,000. Fortunately for the foundation, this was not the first or last gift from the utility company.[3]

Putney's connections with the firm began with his brother, Mark, who retired as chairman and CEO of Midwest Resources Inc., a predecessor of MidAmerican Energy Services, in 1992. Putney maintained ties with key personnel at the utility, and early on, Russell Christiansen, the CEO who followed his brother at the firm, gave the foundation $100,000 on behalf of the company. Later, Putney got to know Greg Abel, president and CEO of MidAmerican Energy Holdings Company (renamed Berkshire Hathaway Energy; MidAmerican Energy Services is one of its subsidiaries) through Bill Knapp, who introduced Abel and Putney at one of his fair campsite dinners. In 2007, the growing relationship bore fruit for the fair. The company had been building wind turbines in Iowa since Governor Tom Vilsack's renewable energy initiative in 2003, and a month after sitting Governor Chet Culver followed this up with a sustainable energy plan of his own in March 2007, MidAmerican announced plans to double its production of wind-generated energy across the state. Included in the expansion was a planned 133-foot wind turbine for the Iowa State Fairgrounds, which would not only generate electricity but highlight the significance of wind energy in Iowa. Along with the turbine, MidAmerican pledged $1 million to the Blue Ribbon Foundation over a ten-year period.[4]

The wind turbine and a temporary MidAmerican visitor's center with displays on renewable energy went up on Expo Hill in time for the 2007 fair, with the company building a permanent education center two years later (now renamed the MidAmerican Education Center). Tom Budler, MidAmerican Energy's general manager of wind development, expressed the company's satisfaction with the outreach center, saying, "The fair is a great opportunity to educate customers and Iowans in general about wind energy." Putney, Slater, and the Fair Board were happy as well; the budding relationship with MidAmerican was proving good for the fair.[5]

Putney remained in close contact with Greg Abel and Bill Fehrman, CEO of MidAmerican Energy, after the Expo Hill project was completed. Soon both Abel and Fehrman were thinking about ways to attract more fairgoers to MidAmerican's displays up on the hill. Abel, Fehrman, and Putney looked at the old Fairview Stage, located just southwest of the MidAmerican Energy Education Center. The fair's long-range plans called for its redevelopment and expansion. Putney told Scott Worth he had a potential donor interested in redoing the stage and needed preliminary drawings of what the new one might look like. By the end of 2013, Putney had a MidAmerican pledge of $1.5 million for the project, but the estimated cost of the new stage was about $4 million, and he had to convince the Fair Board it was a worthwhile endeavor to pursue immediately.[6]

Although the large donation would be lost if the board did not go forward with the new entertainment venue, some board members saw this as a case of donor interest determining which improvements were undertaken. But Putney's argument that the stage was already on their list of desired upgrades and would soon need to be replaced convinced the board to go forward with the project. Completed for the 2015 fair, the MidAmerican Energy Stage featured a larger stage, an expanded seating area, dressing rooms, restrooms, and a loading dock. But the most noticeable architectural feature Worth incorporated into the new free entertainment venue was its roof, which he came up with while bending and twisting a drink coaster. Shaped in the words of KCCI newsman Steve Karlin "like a bird in flight," the steel-and-concrete-framed "wings" spread gracefully over the new stage.[7]

Putney had similar success bringing in another big donor for a project that was also not in the Fair Board's immediate plans. For years he had been trying to involve the Ruans, a wealthy Des Moines family whose fortune was based on trucking, banking, and real estate, in the fair. Putney's brother, Mark, had introduced him to John Ruan, the family patriarch and founder of the companies, and Putney began building a relationship with him because the Blue Ribbon's office was first located in Two Ruan Center, where he often saw the business leader. Later, Ruan's son, John III, who was in the process of taking over leadership of the family's companies, discounted the foundation's rent when it moved into larger offices in the Ruan Center. Putney took advantage of Ruan being named an "Iowan of the Day" in 1998 by showing him around the fairgrounds and discussing needed restorations. He continued courting Ruan, but he never found a fair project that appealed to the aging trucking magnate, who died in 2010.[8]

But patience and persistence had always characterized Putney's fund-raising approach. As Ruan's health declined, Putney began cultivating John III and his wife, Janis. By that time Janis in particular had become a leading figure in the beautification of Des Moines, initially focusing on the "gateways" to downtown, Fleur Drive to the south and Ingersoll Avenue to the west. She was also especially active in renovation and expansion of the Greater Des Moines Botanical Garden.[9]

In 2010, after several years sporadically visiting John III and Janis, Putney and his wife, Emily, were invited to a Knapp dinner party at the fair that included the Ruans. Putney offered the couple a golf cart tour of the fairgrounds, focusing on the recently completed Jacobson Center. He knew of their involvement in beautification and thought he might have a project between the new arena and the Varied Industries Building that would interest them. Ever since the 2004 master plan was created, fair officials had been considering an east–west pedestrian avenue cutting midway through the fairgrounds, designed to relieve traffic on its main thoroughfares of Grand Concourse and Rock Island Avenue. Connecting to this from the north was a broad sidewalk from the Varied Industries Building that meandered south toward what had been the covered arena.[10]

The proposed landscaped walkway was similar to work Janis had headed in Des Moines, and Putney believed it would appeal to the couple. He was especially interested in showing them the north–south portion of the plan and had been discussing it with fair manager Gary Slater. As the *Register* reported the following year, the idea was "to create a park-like plaza as a thoroughfare leading from the Grand Concourse, on the east side of the Varied Industries Building, straight south to the [new] Richard O. Jacobson Exhibition Center." Putney told John III and Janis about the concept and showed them where it would be located. Later, as was his penchant, Putney asked Scott Worth to come up with some preliminary drawings and showed them to John III, who liked what he saw.[11]

The plans called for a three-part project beginning with the north–south mall Putney had described to the *Register*. This would consist of two parallel tree-lined paved walkways, situated between the Des Moines Register Service Center and the Varied Industries Building running south from the Grand Concourse toward the Jacobson Center. The walkways were to be separated by lush greenspace, which included improved drainage and new utilities for vendors, cleaning up and beautifying an area often plagued with mud. Phases two and three would extend the plaza through the machinery grounds southeast of the Varied Industries Building, providing "distinct pedestrian and parking areas" before turning west and reaching gate ten of the fairgrounds.[12]

The Ruans were pleased with the design and in 2011 pledged $750,000 toward the project with the understanding that it would not go forward immediately because they had other commitments. Further plans for the esplanade were developed with estimated costs at roughly $4 million. Putney and Slater then went to the board and pressed the case for the plaza. But the project was not on the Fair Board's capital campaign plan, and many board members were resistant because the Ruans' commitment was well short of covering the costs. Some wondered if the expensive mall would really add value for the fairgoer. The discussion dragged on for three years before the board finally gave it a green light in 2014.[13]

Construction started after that year's exhibition, with phase one of Ruan Plaza completed for the 2015 fair. This went a long way toward improving that portion of the fairgrounds. Board member Jerry Parkin described the impact of the new walkway as "absolutely huge," while Scott Worth remembered feeling gratified that "everyone, board members, staff, everyone, loved it." The Ruans were impressed as well and donated an additional $250,000 toward the pedestrian mall.[14]

While Putney was pushing for Ruan Plaza, he was also talking with Sheri Horner. Bob and Sheri Horner had been generous donors over the years, most notably funding the installation of the fountain at the fairgrounds' Legacy Terrace. Bob's health was declining, and Sheri wanted to do "something significant" to honor him at the fair. Putney came up with several possible projects. One called for redoing the fairgrounds' main gate at Grand Avenue. But there was concern that Bob might not live long enough to see something that required construction. It then occurred to Putney that the highly visible Des Moines Register Service Center (formerly known as the Firstar Service Center) across the Grand Concourse from the Grandstand was always associated with a sponsorship, and he could offer the couple naming rights for $500,000. The Horners liked the building's central location and the turn-key aspect of the project. They wrote the check, which could be used toward any fair renovation. The building was renamed the Robert G. Horner and Sheri Avis Horner Service Center in 2013, and Sheri brought Bob out to see it and have his photo taken in front of it before he passed away the following year.[15]

The gift put the total raised by the Putney-led Blue Ribbon Foundation at $95 million during his twenty-year tenure, but his retirement was now near. His passion for the fair and his ability to convey that to others, combined with his perseverance while working with potential donors, had paid off big time, providing funds for fair officials to erect or renovate thirty buildings since 1993. Slater knew how important Putney had been to the fair's turnaround and asked him if "he wanted to re-up the contract" and stay in the job. He understood that Putney's connections and aptitude for building relationships were central to his achievement at the foundation. Contributor Denny Elwell agreed, explaining that Putney's "knack for making people feel good about donating and working with those around him to deploy those donations" had been essential to rebuilding the fairgrounds.[16]

Although Putney still loved the fair and remained zealous about selling it to others, he was ready to return full-time to his cattle business and declined Slater's offer. The two began discussing the foundation's prospects and a new director. Putney was sanguine that once they found the right person, the impending transition would be smooth. Most important, he had great faith in Robin (Lage) Taylor, who had been with him since 1999. As the Blue Ribbon Foundation's assistant director, she handled day-to-day operations and current programs—including its new fund-raiser, the Fairgrounds 5K Run, added in 2007—with aplomb. She was, Putney noted, "a great number two," who, he knew, "would provide stability and continuity for the foundation into the future." He had similar confidence in the rest of his staff, Jenna Beary, the sponsorship director, and Drew Norton, the communications manager, who he thought rounded out an "outstanding team."[17]

Putney and Slater talked for months about filling the executive director's slot, but it was Emily Putney who first suggested a potential successor to her husband: Peter Cownie, a successful young man who Putney thought "was well-connected, had a great demeanor, was politically savvy, and could relate to the up-and-coming business and community leaders around the state." He also happened to be the youngest son of two of the biggest fair supporters, Jim and Patty Cownie.[18]

A Des Moines native, Cownie had attended Dowling Catholic High School in West Des Moines before going to the University of Virginia. While there, he interned for Iowa Senator Chuck Grassley and in the White House before graduating in 2003 with a bachelor's degree in American government. He soon took a job at the Department of Transportation in Washington, DC, where he stayed three years before deciding to return to Des Moines and pursue a career in politics. Putney met with the twenty-five-year-old Cownie, was impressed with his background, and helped him get a job working for the Iowa Senate Republican Caucus staff. Here he served as a legislative analyst for committees on state government and health and human services, and it was here that Putney, a Republican state senator at the time, came to know Cownie as a bright and conscientious person who understood how to work with people.[19]

During his time at the Iowa Statehouse, Cownie also went to Drake University and received his master's degree in public administration. A year and a half later, in January 2008, he landed a job as the executive director of Junior Achievement of Central Iowa, but his interest in politics remained, and he ran for a seat in the Iowa legislature that November and won. The Putneys continued to see Cownie and follow his successes until summer 2012, when they agreed he was the right person to follow Putney at the foundation. Putney went to see Slater and told him, "I've got an idea. There is a young man named Peter Cownie out there who has all the ingredients to head the foundation. He has the passion and the personality we need." Slater shared Putney's enthusiasm for Cownie.[20]

That fall, the Putneys took Peter and his wife, Mary, to dinner, where Putney raised the issue of his pending retirement and asked if Peter would be interested in heading the foundation. Peter said yes on the spot. Putney and Slater began talking through the details, and the following spring 2013, they went to the Fair Board, where Putney explained that he was planning to step down and that Peter Cownie had all the right tools to succeed him at the foundation. When Putney finished speaking, Jerry Parkin exclaimed, "That's a great idea; I think Peter Cownie will be wonderful." Others immediately followed suit in expressing their approval, and the board recommended that Slater offer Cownie the job. He did, and Cownie accepted.[21]

Cownie started at the foundation in August 2013, with Putney remaining in place until the following March to familiarize his successor with the fair and foundation. Unbeknownst to Putney, one of Cownie's first duties was to get the outgoing executive director to attend that fair's opening ceremony the morning of August 8. There, in front of the Cattle Barn, Slater and the Fair Board had a surprise waiting for Putney. To recognize him for his outstanding work, they had renamed the Cattle Barn in his family's honor.[22]

It was the ideal gift; the building held great significance for Putney because of his years in the cattle business, his service as the fair's beef superintendent, and his time as president of the Sale of Champions. But Putney had not planned on attending the event because he was busy with the fair's opening, and it was only Cownie's arm-twisting that brought him to the ceremony. Once there, Putney was completely caught off guard when the new sign atop the building was uncovered, rechristening it the John and Emily Putney Family Cattle Barn. He was overwhelmed; his name would now be immortalized at the fairgrounds he so loved and had been instrumental in rebuilding. "I was shocked," he said. As *Register* reporter Kyle Munson noted later in the day, Putney was "still shaking his head in disbelief as he zipped around the fairgrounds in his golf cart."[23]

Putney camped at the Blue Ribbon Foundation compound and entertained guests there one last time at the 2013 fair, and as he always did with his wife, Emily, closed out the eleven-day event by riding the Ye Old Mill on the last evening of the exhibition.

Undoubtedly Putney's retirement was leaving very large shoes to fill, but he felt good about the organization's prospects. "The future is bright for the Iowa State Fair," Putney said, "and the Blue Ribbon Foundation will continue to flourish under the leadership of an outstanding individual, Peter Cownie."[24]

The transition was made much easier because Cownie understood the responsibility he had undertaken and planned to listen and learn. He saw himself as a sponge, "attempting to soak up as much knowledge as possible" from Putney, Slater, and others who had made the fair and foundation such a success. At the same time, many believed Cowie was similar to the outgoing director. He was, according to assistant director Robin Taylor, "cut from the same cloth as John [Putney]." Slater saw Cownie in the similar vein. He shared Putney's patience and leadership abilities and his skills in working with people, and had a large network of connections. And he thought that although Cownie did not possess Putney's agricultural background or long tie to the fair, he understood that "agriculture is the backbone of the fair," which Slater saw as the critical element "that sets us apart from [amusement parks like] Adventureland."[25]

Equally as important, Putney had laid the groundwork for several large donations, some of them from donors he had, not surprisingly, met through Knapp. He had spent years building a relationship with Bob Pulver, founder and CEO of All-State Industries, a West Des Moines-based manufacturer of conveyor belts and other nonmetallic machine parts, and his wife, Deb. It was Knapp who had first sent Deb, an interior designer, to see Putney about doing some work at the fair. The Putneys and the Pulvers soon became good friends and began spending time together at the fair. Bob Pulver kept telling Putney he "wanted to do something for the fair," and in 2013 he stated that he would make a commitment before Putney stepped down. The two couples attended the last Grandstand concert at that year's fair together, and Putney reminded Pulver of his promise and joked, "Heck, there's only a couple of hours left, Bob." Pulver replied that he had not forgotten, and at the end of the last song, he told Putney that he and Deb would give the Blue Ribbon Foundation $1 million. The relocated outdoor arena just east of the Swine Barn is now named in their honor.[26]

Similarly, Putney was introduced to Denny and Susan Albaugh and Mark and Jill Oman through Knapp, meeting them, like the Ruans, at Knapp dinner parties at the fair. Albaugh, the founder and owner of Albaugh Inc., a leading producer and packager of agrochemical products, told Putney as early as 2005 that he would make a significant contribution to the fair when he sold his company. The firm's sale, which had been arranged in 2010, fell through, but Putney and Albaugh kept talking. In the meantime, Putney was also becoming acquainted with Mark Oman, a close friend of Knapp's and senior vice president at Wells Fargo, who headed the bank's home lending and consumer finance operations based in West Des Moines. He also happened to be the brother of David Oman, who had worked with the Fair Board to establish the Blue Ribbon Foundation and, along with Bill Riley, headed it briefly before Putney was hired. Mark and his wife, Jill, were becoming more interested in the fair, and Putney kept in close touch. As he had done with the Albaughs, Putney gave the Omans tours of the grounds, VIP parking, free admission, and tickets to concerts and special events.[27]

Neither couple committed to the foundation on Putney's watch, but he clearly had piqued their interest. It was Cownie who picked up where Putney left off and closed the deals. Each couple pledged $1 million to the fair in 2015. That same year, Cownie enjoyed two more big successes, bringing in million-dollar gifts from Kyle Krause, president and CEO of Krause Gentle Corporation, owner of Kum & Go convenience stores, and his wife, Sharon, and Mary Andringa, board chair of the Vermeer Corporation, and her husband, Dr. Dale Andringa. Although both couples had been courted by Putney, it was Cownie who continued pursuing them, and it was the new executive director who was ultimately responsible for these last two gifts.[28]

Like big donors such as the Elwells and the Cownies, some of these new contributors were interested in camping at the fair, and the Blue Ribbon Foundation and Gary Slater accommodated them, setting up a second VIP campsite east of the Cultural Center and south of Grandfather's Barn. There the Albaughs, the Andringas, the Krauses, and the Omans rolled up in luxury motor homes and enjoyed the 2015 fair.[29]

Just as the mantle of leadership was being passed to Cownie in March 2014, the ubiquitous Bill Knapp entered the mix with a big idea. He had been down to Simpson College in Indianola to see the twenty-five-foot "God Bless America" statue, artist Seward Johnson's oversized homage to Grant Wood's famous American Gothic painting, which the institution's Iowa History Center had hosted on campus since the previous June. When Knapp saw the giant couple, he exclaimed, "I want that! I want that at the Iowa State Fair! Can you imagine how perfect that would be?"[30]

He immediately inquired about the statue and learned its six-month rental fee was $30,000 and that it was about to be dismantled and returned to the artist's studio in New Jersey. He quickly called Peter Cownie to ask about the fair's interest in the statue and then called the artist's foundation about the possibility of moving it to the fairgrounds. Fair officials were indeed interested, and Cownie and Slater came to see the statue a few days later. Knapp then called Cownie's father, Jim, and asked his friend to split the cost of renting the statue with him and bring it to the Iowa State Fair. Jim Cownie agreed, and a week later the statue was taken down. Its components were loaded onto two semitrailers for the short trip north from the college to the fairgrounds, where it was installed in a central location on Rock Island Avenue in front of Pella Plaza.[31]

The statue's stay "was a huge hit with fairgoers," noted Lori Chappell, then the marketing director at the fair. Indeed, it was a perfect pairing, bringing together Iowa's most iconic figures and the state's renowned cultural treasure. That summer over one million people, a third of the state's entire population, marveled at the colossal stern farmer and his daughter as they gazed across the crowds of the 155th annual Iowa State Fair.[32]

With the grand statue overseeing the grounds, Cownie began his first year heading the foundation on his own. Because Putney had enjoyed such success raising funds for the restoration of the run-down fairgrounds, Cownie's mission at the foundation was slightly different. He was charged with building the endowment fund established to maintain its facilities and working with the Fair Board and staff to keep the Iowa State Fair vibrant and attractive to current and future patrons.

Cownie understood the importance of the endowment and strove to grow the fund, but he soon found the job challenging. "People like to give toward projects," he noted, "and the naming rights we offer here at the Iowa State Fair prove a powerful inducement for major gifts." Still, the endowment consisted of roughly $500,000 by 2016, and Cownie had a long-term goal of raising $20 million for the fund, which would provide $1 million annually and cover the operating expenses of the foundation.[33]

More immediately, Cownie, Slater, and the Fair Board began identifying the fair's greatest needs as they strove to stay ahead of the demands of twenty-first century fairgoers. Their discussions soon turned to the Grandstand and Midway areas. Eventually a $30 million three-phase project was developed, which would be the largest capital improvement ever undertaken by the fair.

First on the list was a revamped Midway to be ready for the 2017 fair. The enlarged and reconfigured amusement zone would be paved, receive new utilities, and be extended northwest into a portion of the racetrack. Because the track needed to be removed, auto racing was suspended, and ground was broken for the project shortly after the 2016 fair. The other big change involved the Midway's operation. For years the fair had contracted with entertainment companies, most recently Belle City Amusements, to provide rides and oversee the venue. But fair officials decided that after the current contract with Belle City expired in 2016, they would manage the Midway themselves. In doing so, fair officials were following the lead of state fairs in Minnesota and Wisconsin, which had already taken over their midways, hoping to provide a better quality experience in its new amusement area while at the same time enjoying a new revenue stream.[34]

Phase two of the project, to be completed for the 2018 fair, focused on the Grandstand and its stage, which was now too small to attract many top entertainers. This concern would be addressed with a new permanent stage, double the size of the present one. It would be moved north onto the grounds that had been occupied by the racetrack, and the Grandstand's seating would be increased by three thousand.[35]

Finally, phase three called for the building of a new track and the return of motor racing to the fairgrounds in 2019. Based on a suggestion from Midwest Racing Promotions, which had overseen auto racing at the fair, the new track would be shortened from the previous track's five-eighths-mile length to the more popular three-eighths-mile oval. The smaller track would sit northwest of the Grandstand stage with a north–south orientation as opposed to the prior track, which ran east to west parallel to the Grandstand. It would accommodate rodeos and tractor pulls as well as racing and have its own set of bleachers, with permanent seating for at least 6,500 people on the west side of the new track.[36]

By 2016, the foundation had raised $7.5 million in private contributions for these updates and sought $10 million from the general assembly, but when its request was only partially funded at $5.5 million, it planned to seek the remainder during the 2017 legislative session.

Cownie, meanwhile, remained especially bullish on the project and saw it as pivotal for the fair in the coming years. "It will go a long way," he believed, "to setting up the financial future of the fair for a long time."[37]

Clearly, modernizing the fair to meet the changing interests and desires of Iowans was critical, and this was but the latest move to do so. The Blue Ribbon Foundation had made such updating possible, but of course the foundation's role had always been much more important than that. Indeed, over its brief existence, the foundation proved indispensable to the Iowa State Fair. It had saved the historic fairgrounds, a principal part of this enduring Iowa tradition. For fair manager Gary Slater, not needing to worry about the now beautifully restored grounds was crucial because it allowed fair officials to devote all their energies to the exhibition itself. "The foundation set us free financially," Slater explained, "and because of that catalyst, the whole fair—board, staff, volunteers, and clientele—can now focus on working together to keep the fair growing. It is the biggest thing that happens in Iowa every year."[38]

CONCLUSION

By the 1960s, the luster had worn off the once grand Iowa State Fairgrounds, and the aging facility seemed to be on life support. Efforts to address its problems and stem the deterioration came to naught, and the decline continued. Some wondered if the fair was a relic of the past that had outlived its usefulness.

In 1988 a fair brochure alerted the public that millions of dollars were needed to repair the damage wrought by time and weather. The fair's turn-of-the-century structures were crumbling. The Horse and Sheep Barns needed new roofs, concrete was falling off the Grandstand, and the floor of the Varied Industries Building was sinking. Likewise, the Agriculture Building's doors and windows were rotting and its brickwork breaking apart, the Administration Building "face[d] architectural condemnation," and because of termite infestation, unless new beams and seats were soon installed in the Livestock Pavilion, the structure would have to be closed. "Full-scale renovation is now critical," the pamphlet warned. "Otherwise, a gradual shutdown of facilities is inevitable."[1]

But the doom and gloom pitch did not work. The public did not step forward, and the legislature was not moved to fill the Fair Board's requests for appropriations. Now desperate, the Fair Board and manager were forced to think creatively, and they established the Blue Ribbon Foundation, pinning the fate of the fair on its ability to raise millions of badly needed dollars. After a sluggish start, the foundation took off in 1993 when John Putney was tapped to lead it.

Fair manager and CEO Gary Slater noted that Putney brought a new attitude to the table. He put a positive spin on the fund-raising effort. "He said heck with the negative stuff. Let's not talk about our problems, let's talk about our future, and let's talk about our success. Let's talk about...why the Iowa State Fair is the biggest thing every year, and let's ask people to join us rather than asking them to bail us out." Simply put, Putney and the foundation invited Iowans to be part of the fair's success. The change in tone was soon clear, as the grim 1988 fair brochure entitled "A Proud Iowa Tradition Crumbles in Distress" gave way to the foundation's first fund-raising campaign called "Treasure Our Fair."[2]

Iowans heeded Putney's call to save their fair and contributed to donor programs designed for every pocketbook. Corporations and the legislature opened their checkbooks as well, and money began pouring into the foundation's coffers. Restoration of the fairgrounds began almost immediately.

The Blue Ribbon Foundation was making significant progress, but it got a game-changing boost when Putney won over real estate developer and philanthropist Bill Knapp in 1997. Fair Board member Paul Vaassen went so far as to joke that Putney's success was tied to "getting to know Bill Knapp." In a sense, though, there was a lot of truth to the statement. Many have come to know Knapp, fewer have become good friends with him, and fewer still were able to get Knapp to donate millions to their cause. Putney scored on all three counts. Even better, he inspired Knapp to make the fair a cause of his own. Knapp introduced many of his wealthy friends to the fair, spoke out on the fair's behalf, and convinced others to give. Unquestionably, Knapp's significance to the fair went well beyond his donations. Putney himself believed that nearly $30 million in contributions and state appropriations to the fair came in because of Knapp's involvement.[3]

Knapp notwithstanding, Slater explained Putney's success more broadly: "John saw an opportunity to sell the tradition and greatness of the fair to those who had the means and influence to make a difference. John reminded all that the classic American State Fair was here, right under our noses."[4]

After a decade of the foundation's fund-raising efforts, the Iowa State Fair had undergone an astonishing $53 million face-lift. The *Des Moines Register*'s Rox Laird, who had followed the fair closely since 1991, applauded: "The historic buildings have been rescued from physical decay, and the fairgrounds have been transformed into a handsome showcase for the best Iowa has to offer. The place was a disgrace just over a decade ago, and it's hard to say how much longer fans, exhibitors and concessionaires would have put up with conditions. Today, other states are studying Iowa's success story with envy."[5]

Indeed, according to Don Greiman, a former longtime Fair Board member, the Iowa State Fair had never drawn much interest from other state fairs until the foundation rejuvenated the fairgrounds. Then fair officials from around the country were regular visitors, coming to see how Iowa had revived its fair. Once here, Greiman recalled, such representatives "could not believe our facilities—those grand old facilities and how we kept them. They also talk[ed] about the new facilities we're building and how they blend in." Greiman was most impressed, though, by the comment of a past president of the International Association of Fairs and Expositions, who gave the Iowa State Fair high marks: "It smells, it sounds, and it looks like a state fair ought to."[6]

Beth (Reinig) Greiner, the foundation's first assistant director, explained Putney's success: "He blended his passion for fair traditions with his business and political skills to ignite a movement in the state where individuals, legislators, and corporations all wanted to be a part of ensuring a bright future for the grand tradition of the Iowa State Fair."[7]

When the restoration process of the fair wound down, improvements and expansion followed, making the Iowa State Fair bigger and better. The crusade to preserve and enhance the fairgrounds continues unabated. Peter Cownie, the current head of the Blue Ribbon Foundation, appreciated that "Iowans have made the Iowa State Fair what it is today" and pledged to follow in Putney's footsteps and work with people from all around the state to preserve and enrich Iowa's "time-honored summer tradition."[8]

As he looked to the future, Cownie saw nothing but possibilities, "limited only by [the fairground's] real estate." But he also understood what Putney knew so well, that the Iowa State Fair linked the past to the present, and the historic grounds were an essential component of the experience. "It is my belief," Cownie observed, "that we should always strive to maintain our history, as those fundamentals are what have made us great, while also implementing new ideas to benefit all fairgoers."[9]

What would have happened to the Iowa State Fair without the Blue Ribbon Foundation? Jan Higgins, former assistant manager of the fair, believed that "Band-Aid" repairs would have continued on the fair's major buildings.[10] But given the years of neglect, such minimal maintenance would not have staved off their ultimate demise, and signature structures such as the Livestock Pavilion, the Agriculture Building, or the Grandstand would soon have faced demolition, much like Exposition Hall and the Women's and Children's Building before them.[11]

The consequences of the continuing decline of the fairgrounds would have been dire, according to Fair Board member Jerry Parkin: "It would have become a mediocre state fair, attracting six hundred thousand to seven hundred thousand people a year, while its buildings continued to crumble." Instead, it is now one of the nation's top-tier fairs, annually attracting more than a million patrons to its well-kept facilities, the epitome of a classic American fairground.

For Iowans, though, the foundation's importance lay elsewhere; it had preserved and maintained an essential part of the state's heritage and tradition. Here at their fairgrounds, people from all across the state and all walks of life will continue to convene, as they have for generations, at their annual summer reunion, where, as the *Des Moines Register* once explained, "We are not Cyclone or Hawk, urban or rural, newcomer or lifer. We are Iowans." Some will eat corndogs, watch livestock competitions, learn of the latest agricultural equipment, or see a Grandstand show. Others might stroll through the animal barns, listen to barkers hawking gadgets in the Varied Industries Building, try a Midway ride, view the Butter Cow, marvel at the Big Boar, or just gawk at other fairgoers. And thanks to the Blue Ribbon Foundation, here they will celebrate all that is Iowa for generations to come.[12]

A NOTE ON SOURCES

This book is based on a wide variety of public and private sources, which are listed throughout the endnotes. Of the former, I made extensive use of material from the fair's founding organization, the Iowa State Agricultural Society; annual volumes of the Iowa Department of Agriculture's *Iowa Yearbook of Agriculture*; and records, papers, and plans of the Iowa State Fair, the Iowa State Fair Board, and the Iowa State Fair Blue Ribbon Foundation. The *Des Moines Register* (and its precursor newspapers), which closely covered the Iowa State Fair, was likewise essential to this study as were several books about the fair, particularly those by Mary Kay Shanley, Thomas Leslie, and Chris Rasmussen, already mentioned in the acknowledgments. Especially helpful were a number of individuals who sat for interviews, corresponded with me, and/or gave me access to their private papers. A list of these people and their contributions follows.

Manuscript Collections
Greiner, Beth, Papers. Private Collection, Omaha, Nebraska.
Laird, Rox, Papers. Private Collection, Des Moines, Iowa.
Overton, Chip, Papers. Private Collection, West Des Moines, Iowa.
Parkin, Jerry, Papers. Private Collection, Earlham, Iowa.
Putney, John, Papers. Private Collection, Gladbrook, Iowa.
Swift, Kathie, Papers. Private Collection, West Des Moines, Iowa.
Vaassen, Paul, Papers. Private Collection, Dubuque, Iowa.
Zeller, John, Papers. Private Collection, Des Moines, Iowa.

Interviews and Correspondence with Author
Balko, Grafton. Correspondence with author, 11 January 2016.
Boesen, Connie. Interview by author, Des Moines, Iowa, 20 April 2015.
Cownie, Jim. Interview by author, Des Moines, Iowa, 17 September 2012.
   Correspondence with author, 28 January, 2 February 2016.

Cownie, Peter. Interviews by author, Des Moines, Iowa, 19 February,
    18 October 2016. Correspondence with author, 16 May 2016.

Elwell, Denny. Interview by author, Ankeny, Iowa, 19 July 2016.

Finch, Bobbie. Telephone conversation with author, 15 July 2015.

Fisher, Carly. Correspondence with author, 18 February 2016.

Fuson, Ken. Correspondence with author, 5 January 2016.

Greiman, Don. Telephone conversation with author, 27 April 2015.

Greiner, Beth. Telephone conversation with author, 12 June 2015.
    Correspondence with author, 15 December 2015.

Higgins, Jan. Interview by author, Pleasant Hill, Iowa, 2 June 2015.
    Telephone coversation with author, 5 November 2015.

Horner, Sheri. Telephone conversation with author, 31 December 2015.

Knapp, Bill. Interviews by author, West Des Moines, Iowa, 24 August 2012;
    20 January 2016.

Knapp, Susan. Inverviews by author, Van Meter and West Des Moines,
    Iowa, 5 October 2012; 20 January 2016. Correspondence with author,
    4 December 2015.

Lock, Joyce. Telephone conversation with author, 11 December 2015.

Lucas, Marion. Telephone conversation with author, 12 May 2015.

Miller, Amy. Interview by author, West Des Moines, Iowa,
    18 November 2015. Correspondence with author, 19 November 2015.

Nye, Judy. Telephone conversation with author, 21 August 2015.

Oman, David. Interview by author, Des Moines, Iowa, 25 June 2015.

Parkin, Jerry. Interview by author, Winterset, Iowa, 13 October 2015.

Putney, Emily. Interview by author, Gladbrook, Iowa, 17 August,
    23 October 2015.

Putney, John. Interviews by author, Des Moines and Gladbrook,
    Iowa, 10 July 2012; 8 May, 23 July, 23 October 2015; 9 July
    2016.Correspondence with author, 5 January, 29 April, 9 May,
    25, 26 October 2016. Telephone conversation with author,
    18 February 2016.

Roland, Judy. Telephone conversation with author, 14 September 2015.

Schlutz, Bob. Interview by author, Des Moines, Iowa, 17 August 2015.

Slater, Gary. Interview by author, Des Moines, Iowa, 15 January 2016.

Swift, Kathie. Interview by author, West Des Moines, Iowa, 2 July 2015.

Taylor, Jim. Interview by author, Des Moines, Iowa, 17 August 2015.

Taylor, Robin. Interview by author, Des Moines, Iowa, 26 January 2016. Correspondence with author, 10, 16, 19 November 2015; 19 February, 26 October 2016.

Vaassen, Paul. Interview by author, Des Moines, Iowa, 12 August 2015.

Wittmack, Dee. Correspondence with author, 14 December 2015.

Worth, Scott. Interview by author, Des Moines, Iowa, 23 December 2015.

NOTES

INTRODUCTION

1. Chris Rasmussen, *Carnival in the Countryside: The History of the Iowa State Fair* (Iowa City: University of Iowa Press, 2015), 1.
2. See *Wall Street Journal*, 19 July 2002; Patricia Schultz, *1,000 Places to See Before You Die: A Traveler's Life List* (New York: Workman Publishing, 2003), 630; and *Midwest Living* magazine website, http://www.midwestliving.com/travel/around-the-region/30-things-every-midwesterner-should-experience/?page=12, accessed on 8 March 2016.
3. *Des Moines Register*, 11 August 1991.
4. *Blue Ribbon* (Spring 1994): 2, Blue Ribbon Foundation quarterly newsletter, Newsletter Binder, Iowa State Fair Blue Ribbon Foundation Papers, collection held by the Blue Ribbon Foundation, Des Moines, Iowa.
5. Quotation from *Des Moines Register*, 3 August 2003.

CHAPTER 1

1. On early fairs, see Karal Ann Martling, *Blue Ribbon: A Social and Pictorial History of the Minnesota State Fair* (St. Paul: Minnesota Historical Society Press, 1990), 18–19; Earle Ross, "The Iowa State Fair," *Palimpsest* (July 1954): 265; and https://www.fairsandexpos.com/eweb/DynamicPage.aspx?Site=iafe&WebCode=History, accessed on 30 May 2015.
2. *Galland's Iowa Emigrant*, quoted in William Friedricks, *Investing in Iowa: The Life and Times of F. M. Hubbell* (Des Moines: The Iowan Books, 2007), 5; on settlement of Iowa, see Dorothy Schwieder, *Iowa: The Middle Land* (Ames: Iowa State University Press, 1996), 35–40. Population numbers from Leland Sage, *A History of Iowa* (Ames: Iowa State University Press, 1974), 310.

3. For laws to encourage the creation of agricultural societies, see Chris Rasmussen, *Carnival in the Countryside: A History of the Iowa State Fair* (Iowa City: University of Iowa Press, 2015), 15–16; and Myrtle Beinhauer, "The County, District, and State Agricultural Societies of Iowa," *The Annals of Iowa* 20 (Summer 1935), 51–52.

4. Beinhauer, "Agricultural Societies of Iowa," 55–56. Second quotation from Charles Fulton, *History of Jefferson County, Iowa* (Chicago, IL: S. J. Clarke, 1914), 260.

5. For quotation and more on first fair, see Rasmussen, *Carnival in Countryside*, 13; see also Thomas Leslie, *Iowa State Fair: Country Comes to Town* (New York: Princeton Architectural Press, 2007), 32–38.

6. See Ross, "Iowa State Fair," 279; Shaffer quotation from Ross, 280.

7. Leslie, *Iowa State Fair*, 38.

8. Rasmussen, *Carnival in the Countryside*, 16.

9. Leslie, *Iowa State Fair*, 38–39.

10. Quote from *Iowa State Agricultural Society Report, 1875*: 28; for receipts, see p. 29.

11. For a background history of Des Moines, see Ilda Hammer, *The Book of Des Moines* (Des Moines, IA: Board of Education, 1947), 53–67; Orin Dahl, *Des Moines: Capital City* (Tulsa, OK: Continental Heritage Inc., 1978), 27–33; and Will Porter, *Annals of Polk County, Iowa and the City of Des Moines Iowa* (Des Moines, IA: George A. Miller Printing Co., 1898), 171. See also Friedricks, *Investing in Iowa*, 8; and William Friedricks, *Constructing a Legacy: The Weitz Company and the Family Who Built It* (Des Moines, IA: Business Publications Corp., 2015), 14–17.

12. For population numbers, see http://www.iowadatacenter.org/archive/2011/02/citypop.pdf, accessed on 10 September 2013. *Iowa State Register*, 7 September 1864; William Friedricks, *Covering Iowa: The History of the Des Moines Register and Tribune Company, 1849-1985* (Ames: Iowa State University Press, 2000), 22–23.

13. See *Iowa State Register*, 19 January 1870; 25 August 1872; 29 September, 1, 18 November 1874; 12 January 1875; *Iowa State Leader*, 28 September, 7 October 1874; US Department of the Interior, National Register of Historic Places Nomination Form—

Iowa State Fairgrounds, OMB No. 1024-0018, 14 September 1987, "The Development of the Iowa State Fair & Exposition Grounds Background and Selection of Present Site," 10.

14. For population numbers, see http://www.iowadatacenter.org/archive/2011/02/citypop.pdf, accessed on 10 September 2013. Quotation about Des Moines's growth, see *Bushnell's Des Moines Directory, 1884-85* (Des Moines: Iowa Directory and Gazetteer Co., 1884), 31; and for information on railroads into Des Moines, see Barbara Beving Long, *Des Moines and Polk County: Flag on the Prairie* (Northridge, CA: Windsor Publications, 1988), 29.

15. *Iowa State Register*, 7, 15, 20 November, 5, 10 December 1878; 9, 10, 11, 12, 14, 15, 30 January, 5, 19 February, 20 August, 2 September 1879; *Des Moines Register*, 11 August 1999; and see Johnson Brigham, *Des Moines: The Pioneer of Municipal Progress and Reform of the Middle West with the History of Polk County, Iowa* (Chicago: S. J. Clarke, 1911), 1: 287.

16. Attendance from Mary Kay Shanley, *Our State Fair: Iowa's Blue Ribbon Story* (Des Moines: Iowa State Fair Blue Ribbon Foundation, 2000), 24; quotations from Shaffer and receipt figure from *Iowa State Agricultural Society Report, 1879*: 43, 45.

17. Quotation from Rasmussen, 38; see also Beinhauer, "Agricultural Societies of Iowa," 59; and Ross, "Iowa State Fair," 294–95.

18. Shanley, *Our State Fair*, 35. On Hubbell and Polk, see Friedricks, *Investing in Iowa*, 119.

19. Shanley, *Our State Fair*, 30–31; Beinhauer, "Agricultural Societies of Iowa," 59–60; Brigham, *Des Moines*, 1: 303; Hammer, *Des Moines*, 90–91.

20. Ross, "Iowa State Fair," 296.

CHAPTER 2

1. On visiting other fairgrounds, see *Iowa State Register*, 27 June 1885. For more on visits and quotation, see *Iowa State Agricultural Society Report, 1885* (Des Moines: Iowa State Printer, 1886): 69–70.

2. *Iowa State Register*, 27 June 1885.

3. For quotation, see *Iowa State Register*, 27 June 1885. See also *Iowa State Agricultural Society Report, 1885* (Des Moines: Iowa State Printer, 1886): 64, 71.

4. For layout of fairgrounds, see Hackney to Building Committee, Iowa State Agricultural Society, 31 December 1886, in *Iowa State Agricultural Society Report, 1886*: 612–616. On hiring of Hackney, see *Iowa State Agricultural Society Report, 1885*: 625. On the Rock Island and its trains, see *Iowa State Register*, 4 September 1886.

5. For quotation and building of the fairgrounds, see Thomas Leslie, *Iowa State Fair: Country Comes to Town* (New York: Princeton Architectural Press, 2007), 47. See also US Department of the Interior, National Register of Historic Places Nomination Form— Iowa State Fairgrounds, OMB No. 1024-0018, 14 September 1987, "The Development of the Iowa State Fair & Exposition Grounds Background and Selection of Present Site," 14.

6. Leslie, *Iowa State Fair*, 49.

7. *Iowa State Register*, 27 August 1886.

8. Iowa State Fairgrounds National Register Nomination Form, "Development of the Physical Plant," 16.

9. *Iowa State Agricultural Society Report, 1889*: 96.

10. See Dave Elbert, "The Elbert Files: Bring back Seni-Om-Sed," *Business Record*, 19 July 2013, http://www.businessrecord.com/Content/Opinion/Opinion/Article/The-Elbert-Files--Bring-back-Seni-Om-Sed/168/963/59120, accessed on 10 July 2015.

11. For more on the depression of 1893, see Douglas Steeples and David Whitten, *Democracy in Desperation: The Depression of 1893* (Westport, CT: Greenwood Press, 1998).

12. For more on the Columbian Exposition within context of fairs, see Robert Rydell, *All the World's a Fair: Visions of Empire at American International Expositions, 1876-1916* (Chicago: University of Chicago Press, 1985). On working with Seni-Om-Sed to bring in patrons, see Mary Kay Shanley, *Our State Fair: Iowa's Blue Ribbon Story* (Des Moines: State Fair Blue Ribbon Foundation, 2000), 33, 38; and Chris Rasmussen, "Progress and Catastrophe: Public History at the Iowa State Fair, 1854-1946," *The Annals of Iowa* 63 (Fall 2004), 367.

13. On debt, state appropriation, and first quotation, see Myrtle Beinhauer, "The County, District, and State Agricultural Societies of Iowa," *The Annals of Iowa* 20 (Summer 1935), 63. For Fowler following in line with other fair managers, see Chris Rasmussen,

Carnival in the Countryside: The History of the Iowa State Fair (Iowa City: University of Iowa Press, 2015), 104–05; and for Fowler quote, see Shanley, *Our State Fair*, 261.

14. On creating Iowa's White City, see Rasmussen, *Carnival in the Countryside*, 106. For locomotive collision, see Iowa State Fair website, http://www.iowastatefair.org/about-us/history/permanent-home/, accessed on 14 July 2015.

15. On Carpenter plan, see Iowa State Fairgrounds National Register Nomination Form, "Development of the Physical Plant," 24–27. For amphitheater being destroyed and replaced in 1892, see *Iowa State Agricultural Society Report, 1892*: 142–146.

16. Shanley, *Our State Fair*, 261.

17. Rasmussen, *Carnival in the Countryside*, 106.

18. Quotation from Leslie, *Iowa State Fair*, 54. See also *Iowa Yearbook of Agriculture, 1900* (Des Moines: Iowa State Printer, 1901), 171–72; and Rasmussen, *Carnival in the Countryside*, 108.

19. On the 1900 and 1901 fair, see *Iowa State Register*, 30 August 1901.

20. 20 For background on the City Beautiful Movement, see William Wilson, *The City Beautiful Movement* (Baltimore, MD: Johns Hopkins University Press, 1989).

21. For more on City Beautiful Movement in Des Moines and Des Moines Riverfront Civic Center district, see James Jacobsen, "The City Beautiful Movement and City Planning in Des Moines, Iowa, 1892-1938," National Register of Historic Places, Multiple Property Documentation Form, 7 July 1988, http://pdfhost.focus.nps.gov/docs/NRHP/Text/64500184.pdf, accessed on 15 July 2015.

22. Board plans and quote from *Iowa Yearbook of Agriculture, 1902* (1903), 99. See also *Iowa Yearbook of Agriculture, 1902*, 148, 152.

23. *Des Moines Register and Leader*, 20 August 1902.

24. On fair and its success, see *Iowa Yearbook of Agriculture, 1902* (1903), 102. For fair quote, see *Des Moines Register and Leader*, 20 August 1902.

25. First quotation from Leslie, *Iowa State Fair*, 60; second quotation from Iowa State Fair National Register Nomination Form, "Development of the Physical Plant," 29.

26. For quotation and firms invited to submit plans, see *Iowa Yearbook of Agriculture, 1904* (1905), 124–125.
27. Ibid., 126. For more on Smith, see *Des Moines Register and Leader*, 29 May 1916; and for more on Keffer/Overton firm history, see "Oldest Central Iowa Firm Maintains Deep Roots," typescript, Chip Overton Papers, private collection held by Chip Overton, West Des Moines, Iowa.
28. Leslie, *Iowa State Fair*, 66–67.
29. Shanley, *Our State Fair*, 210–213.
30. Quotation from *Iowa Yearbook of Agriculture, 1908* (1909), 130.
31. Ibid., 139–140.
32. *Iowa Yearbook of Agriculture, 1907* (1908), 199–201.
33. For description of facility and Wagner quote, see National Register of Historic Places Nomination Form—Iowa State Fairgrounds, "Iowa Site Inventory, Grandstand and Education Building, Site 13." On dedication to soldiers of World War I and being state's largest building, see Leslie, *Iowa State Fair*, 88.
34. See Iowa State Fairgrounds National Register Nomination Form, "Development of the Physical Plant," 30. For more on Simonds, see Barbara Geiger, *Low-Key Genius: The Life and Work of Landscape-Gardener, O. C. Simonds* (Evanston, IL: Ferme Ornee Press, 2011). See also his own major work, O. C. Simonds, *Landscape-Gardening* (New York: MacMillan Co., 1920).
35. Iowa State Fair National Register Nomination Form, "Development of the Physical Plant," 31–32, and "Statement of Significance," 24.
36. See *Iowa Yearbook of Agriculture, 1911* (1912), 208, 212–214, 222, 230.
37. For description of building, see Shanley, *Our State Fair*, 202; Wagner quotation from Iowa State Fairgrounds National Register Registration Form, "Iowa Site Inventory—Machinery Hall-Varied Industries Building, Site 10."
38. See Rasmussen, *Carnival in the Countryside*, 76–77. On Smith doing building, see *Iowa Yearbook of Agriculture, 1913* (1914), 44.
39. For *Breeder's Gazette* quotation and more information on the building, see *Iowa Yearbook of Agriculture, 1914* (1915), 226. See also Shanley, *Our State Fair*, 234.

40. For some background on Ye Old Mill history, see Kansas State Fair webpage, https://kansasstatefair.com/page.php?id=1428, accessed on 31 July 2015; *Minneapolis-St. Paul* magazine website, http://mspmag.com/Out-And-About/Articles/Features/Ye-Old-Mill/, accessed on 31 July 2015. On Minnesota State Fair getting Ye Old Mill, see *Annual Report of the Minnesota State Agricultural Society for 1915* (Minneapolis, MN: Syndicate Printing, 1916): 32, 45.

41. *Iowa Yearbook of Agriculture, 1920* (1921), 9, 15.

42. Building was listed on National Register of Historic Places in 1987 as part of the Iowa State Fair and Exposition Grounds; in 1991, the building received its own listing on the National Register, see National Register of Historic Places Registration Form—Iowa Fish and Game Pavilion and Aquarium, 1991, http://focus.nps.gov/pdfhost/docs/NRHP/Text/91001836.pdf, accessed on 31 July 2015. See also *Report of the State Fish and Game Warden for the Biennial Period ending 1924* (Des Moines: State of Iowa, 1924), 5051; *Report of State Fish and Game Warden* (1926), 4–5, 9–10; *Report of the State Fish and Game Warden* (1930), 4–5.

43. For quotation, see David Gebhard and Gerald Mansheim, *Buildings of Iowa* (New York: Oxford University Press, 1993), 210. On building, see also *Iowa Yearbook of Agriculture, 1926,* (1927), 320; and *Iowa Yearbook of Agriculture, 1927* (1928), 390, 394.

44. Fair attendance figures are from Earle Ross, "The Iowa State Fair," *Palimpsest* (July 1954): 323; Des Moines's 1930 population was 143,000; see Ilda Hammer, *Book of Des Moines* (Des Moines, IA: Board of Education, 1947), 363.

45. Ross, "Iowa State Fair," 323; and Phil Strong, *State Fair* (New York: Literary Guild, 1932).

46. On Strong's background, see Robert McCown, "Phil Strong's *State Fair*," at University of Iowa Library website, http://www.lib.uiowa.edu/scua/bai/mccown2.htm, accessed on 1 August 2015. For crews filming at fair, see Ross, "Iowa State Fair," 311.

47. Quotation from Rasmussen, *Carnival in the Countryside*, 140.

CHAPTER 3

1. *Des Moines Register and Leader*, 20 August 1902. Rox Laird quotation from *Des Moines Register*, 11 August 1991.
2. Earle Ross, "The Iowa State Fair," *Palimpsest* (July 1954): 311–312, 323–324; "Celebrating the Territorial Centennial," *The Annals of Iowa* 21 (1938), 472–474.
3. US Department of the Interior, National Register of Historic Places Nomination Form—Iowa State Fairgrounds, OMB No. 1024-0018, 14 September 1987, "Iowa Site Inventory, Poultry Building, Site 8, and 4-H Club Building, Youth Inn, Site 20."
4. Mary Kay Shanley, *Our State Fair: Iowa's Blue Ribbon Story* (Des Moines: Iowa State Fair Blue Ribbon Foundation, 2000), 41–42.
5. On centennial fairs, see Thomas Leslie, *Iowa State Fair: Country Comes to Town* (New York: Princeton Architectural Press, 2007), 98, 100; and Chris Rasmussen, *Carnival in the Countryside: The History of the Iowa State Fair* (Iowa City: University of Iowa Press, 2015), 166–67. Attendance figures from Economic Research Associates (ERA), "Long Range Planning for the Iowa State Fair and World Food Exposition," (1968), section 3, 2. A copy of this report is available at Iowa State University Parks Library.
6. On the Cultural Center, see National Register of Historic Places Nomination Form—Iowa State Fairgrounds, "Iowa Site Inventory, Girls 4-H Dormitory, Cultural Center, Site 17." See also http://www.iowahistory.org/statefair/, accessed on 2 October 2015.
7. *Des Moines Tribune*, 18 January 1950; and Leslie, *Iowa State Fair*, 104.
8. For farms increasing in size but number of farmers decreasing, see James Roark et al., *The American Promise: A Compact History*, vol. 2, 4th ed. (Boston and New York: Bedford St. Martin's, 2010), 683.
9. Ibid., 688.
10. Leslie, *Iowa State Fair*, 100–04; and Shanley, *Our State Fair*, 252.
11. See http://www.billrileytalentsearch.com/about/history, accessed on 1 September 2015.
12. On Teen Town, see https://www.iowarocknroll.com/inductees/291/iowa-state-fair-teen-town/, accessed on 3 September 2015; Leslie, *Iowa State Fair*, 116; and Rasmussen, *Carnival in the Countryside*, 167.

13. Shanley, *Our State Fair*, 264; and Don Greiman with Jan Cox, *A Blue Ribbon Life: Memories of the Iowa State Fair* (Des Moines: Iowa State Fair Blue Ribbon Foundation, 2012), 18.

14. *Iowa Official Register* 51 (1965–66), 106; and *Iowa State Fair Newsletter* (May 1968): 1–2.

15. Don Greiman, telephone conversation with author, 27 March 2015; Connie Boesen, interview by author, Des Moines, Iowa, 20 April 2015; *Iowa State Fair Newsletter* (May 1968); and *Des Moines Register*, 21 July 1968.

16. See ERA, "Long Range Planning for the Iowa State Fair," sections 7 and 8. See also *Iowa State Fair Newsletter* (October 1968).

17. Greiman, telephone conversation; Boesen, interview; John Putney, interview by author, Gladbrook, Iowa, 8 May 2015. For quotation, see Greiman, *Blue Ribbon Life*, 20.

18. On Fulk's interest in pari-mutuel betting and horse racing, see Connie Boesen, interview, and hand drawn version of Iowa State Fair newsletter, 1968, done by Kenny Fulk (according to daughter, Connie Boesen), Iowa State Fair Museum, Des Moines, Iowa.

19. Jim Taylor, interview by author, Des Moines, Iowa, 10 August 2015; Kathie Swift, interview by author, West Des Moines, Iowa, 2 July 2015; Greiman, *Blue Ribbon Life*, 29; Shanley, *Our State Fair*, 264–65; and http://www.iowastatefair.org/about-us/history/1980-1989/, accessed on 9 September 2015.

20. Taylor, interview; and *Iowa State Fair Newsletter* (February 1979): 2–3.

21. *Iowa State Fair Newsletter* (February 1979): 1–3.

22. National Register of Historic Places Nomination Form—Iowa State Fairgrounds, "Application History and Methodology," 18–20; and Jan Higgins, interview by author, Pleasant Hill, Iowa, 2 June 2015; and Kathie Swift, interview.

23. Don Greiman, telephone conversation; Kathie Swift, interview; and *Iowa State Fair Newsletter*, (February 1979): 2.

24. Jim Taylor, interview; and *Iowa State Fair, Historic Highlights, 1854-1983*, 13–14, Rox Laird Papers, private collection held by Rox Laird, Des Moines, Iowa [hereafter cited as Rox Laird Papers].

25. *Iowa State Fair Newsletter* (February 1979): 2.

26. See http://www.iowa.gov/irgc/CommChronology.htm, accessed on 18 September 2015.

27. Shanley, *Our State Fair*, 110; Jan Higgins, interview; Judy Roland, telephone conversation with author, 14 September 2015; Iowa State Fair Board meeting minutes, 15 May 1985; 21 May, 18 June, 17 September, 19 November 1986; 21 January, 20 July, 19 October 1987; 22 June 1988. *Des Moines Register*, 14 June 1985; 28 May, 1, 7 June, 30 July, 1 October 1986; 22 January, 8 December 1987; and Iowa Racing and Gaming Commission Annual Reports, 1985–1988, available online at www.iowa.gov/irgc/annualreports.htm, accessed on 19 September 2015.

28. Jim Taylor, interview; Judy Nye, telephone conversation, 21 August 2015; and Iowa State Fair Board minutes; 16 May, 20 June, 13 August 1984; 16 January 1985. Braren quote from Iowa State Fair Board minutes, 6 December 1984.

29. Jim Taylor, interview. Quotation from Judy Nye, telephone conversation.

30. Don Greiman, telephone conversation; Jim Taylor, interview; Marion Lucas, telephone conversation, 12 May 2015; and Iowa State Fair Board minutes, 8 January 1986.

31. "Iowa State Fair Relocation Study, January 1988," Iowa State Fair Blue Ribbon Foundation Papers, Iowa State Fair, Des Moines, Iowa.

32. *Iowa State Fair Newsletter* (October 1988): 1. For raising more than $25,000, see *Iowa State Fair Newsletter* (January 1989): 2.

33. *Iowa State Fair Newsletter* (October 1988): 1. On hiring of Gene Kennedy, see Iowa State Fair Board minutes, 19 October 1988; and for funding falling short and repair priorities, see *Iowa State Fair Newsletter* (January–February 1991): 1.

34. *Iowa State Fair Newsletter* (January–February 1991): 1.

35. Paul Vaassen, interview by author, Des Moines, Iowa, 12 August 2015. In Nebraska, the foundation and fair struggled. The foundation had only sixty annual donors as late as 2009, and the fair's situation had become so desperate that officials took the drastic step of relocating the exhibition from Lincoln, Nebraska, to Grand Island, Nebraska, in 2010. See *Grand Island* (Nebraska) *Independent*, 13 July 2011.

36. Iowa State Fair Board minutes, 17 January 1991.

37. Iowa State Fair Board minutes, 18 June, 17 July 1991; Stephen Reno to Marion Lucas, 27 December 1990; and Robert Smith to Bobbie Finch, 10 July 1991, both in Paul Vaassen Papers, private collection held by Paul Vaassen, Dubuque, Iowa [hereafter cited as Paul Vaassen Papers].

38. *Des Moines Register*, 11 August 1991.

39. Quote from Bill Riley to Bobbie Finch, Dave Oman, Dave Huniker, Paul Vaassen, and Marion Lucas, 3 November 1991, Paul Vaassen Papers. See also Bill Riley, agenda for Iowa State Fair Foundation members, 19 November 1991, Paul Vaassen Papers; and David Oman, interview by author, Des Moines, Iowa, 25 June 2015.

40. John Putney, interview, 8 May 2015; Robert Schlutz, interview by author, Des Moines, Iowa, 17 August 2015.

41. Ibid.

42. On the Blue Ribbon weekend, see *Des Moines Register*, 17, 24 May 1992; Kathie Swift, interview; Blue Ribbon Weekend news release, 10 April 1992, Kathie Swift Papers, private collection held by Kathie Swift, West Des Moines, Iowa; and Iowa State Fair Board minutes, 17 June 1992.

43. *Des Moines Register*, 13 September 1992.

44. Ibid., 20 November 1992. See also Marion Lucas, telephone conversation; Paul Vaassen, interview; and Kathie Swift, interview.

45. Iowa State Fair Board minutes, 16 December 1992.

46. John Putney, interviews, 8 May, 23 July 2015; Marion Lucas, telephone conversation; Paul Vaassen, interview; and *Des Moines Register*, 5, 6 January 1993.

47. *Des Moines Register*, 20 December 1992.

CHAPTER 4

1. Rox Laird notes of interview with Marion Lucas, 17 December 1992, Rox Laird Papers, private collection held by Rox Laird, Des Moines, Iowa [hereafter cited as Rox Laird Papers]. See also *Des Moines Register*, 20 December 1992. Barnes & Noble story and quotation from John Putney, interview by author, Gladbrook, Iowa, 8 May 2015.

2. Quotation from *Des Moines Register*, 6 January 1993.

3. Iowa State Fair Board meeting minutes, 9 October 1991; Bill Riley, agenda notes for foundation committee meeting, 18 September 1991, Paul Vaassen Papers, private collection held by Paul Vaassen, Dubuque, Iowa [hereafter cited as Paul Vaassen Papers]. See also Paul Vaassen, interview by author, Des Moines, Iowa, 12 August 2015; and John Putney, interviews, 8 May, 23 July 2015. Quotation from Bob Schlutz, interview by author, Des Moines, Iowa, 17 August 2015.

4. Beth Greiner, telephone conversation with author, 12 June 2015; John Putney, interview, 8 May 2015.

5. Jerry Parkin, interview by author, Winterset, Iowa, 13 October 2015.

6. Ibid. See also John Putney, interview, 23 July 2015; Paul Vaassen, interview; Bob Schlutz, interview; Beth Greiner, telephone conversation; Iowa State Fair Board meeting minutes, 17 March 1993; and *Des Moines Register*, 30 March 1993.

7. John Putney to Rox Laird and Dennis Ryerson, 15 February 1993, Rox Laird Papers.

8. John Putney, interview, 23 October 2015.

9. Quote from Vaassen, interview. On tax check off, see David Oman memo, Paul Vaassen Papers; John Putney, interview, 8 May 2015; and *Des Moines Register*, 19 February 1993. On Chickadee Checkoff, see http://www.iowadnr.gov/Environment/WildlifeStewardship/NonGameWildlife/InsideWildlifeDiversity/HowisDiversityFunded/ChickadeeCheckoff.aspx, accessed on 12 October 2015.

10. *Blue Ribbon* (Summer 1994): 1, Blue Ribbon Foundation's quarterly newsletter, first issue, Newsletter Binder, Iowa State Fair Blue Ribbon Foundation Papers, collection held by Blue Ribbon Foundation, Des Moines, Iowa. See also John Putney, interview, 8 May 2015; *Des Moines Register*, 27 April 1993; 28 February 2015: Iowa State Fair Blue Ribbon Foundation fact sheet, Beth Greiner Papers, private collection held by Beth Greiner, Omaha, Nebraska [hereafter referred to as Beth Greiner Papers].

11. *Blue Ribbon* (Summer 1994): 1; and *Des Moines Register*, 5 May 1993.

12. *Des Moines Register*, 5 May 1993.
13. John Putney, interviews, 8 May, 23 July 2015; Beth Greiner, telephone conversation; and *Inside Iowa State*, 28 May 1993, a newsletter for Iowa State University faculty and staff; copy of article from John Putney Papers, private collection held by John Putney, Gladbrook, Iowa [hereafter cited as John Putney Papers].
14. John Putney, interview, 23 July 2015.
15. For original lists of prospects for Iowa State Fair Blue Ribbon Foundation Advisory Board, see Paul Vaassen Papers; and for board members, see Iowa State Fair Blue Ribbon Foundation Kick-Off program, 3 June 1993, John Putney Papers.
16. Jerry Parkin, interview.
17. Muhm quotation from *Des Moines Register*, 4 June 1993; Putney quotation and story about proofs from Jerry Parkin, interview. See also "A Blue Ribbon Story," commemorative book put together in 2014 by Blue Ribbon Foundation for Putney's retirement, John Putney Papers.
18. John Putney, interview, 23 July 2015.
19. Ibid.; and Emily Putney, interview by author, Gladbrook, Iowa, October 23, 2015.
20. Ibid.
21. *Blue Ribbon* (Summer 1994): 3; and John Putney, interview, 23 October 2015.
22. Ibid.
23. John Putney, interview, 23 October 2015. On Putney's intensity and passion for fair, see Amy Miller, interview by author, West Des Moines, Iowa, 18 November 2015.
24. First quotation and information on McNarney from John Putney, interview, 10 July 2012. See also *Des Moines Register*, 14 August 1993; *Blue Ribbon* (Fall 1994): 1, 5–6. Second quotation from *Blue Ribbon* (Fall 2006): 1.
25. Quotation and information on Putney coming up with ideas from Beth Greiner, telephone conversation.
26. On brick program, see *Blue Ribbon* (Spring 1994): 3. For quote about brick, see *Des Moines* Register, 13 February 2002.

27. On success of brick campaign, see Rox Laird notes of interview with John Putney, 8 August 1995, Rox Laird Papers. On Trees Fair-ever campaign, see *Blue Ribbon* (Summer 1995): 3; and Iowa State Fair Blue Ribbon Foundation press release, 12 July 1995, Rox Laird Papers. On name change, see *Blue Ribbon* (Fall 1995): 3; and John Putney, correspondence with author, 9 May 2016. For the Have a Seat program, see *Blue Ribbon* (Summer 1996): 1.

28. For trip, see Iowa State Fair Board minutes, 17 March, 11 June 1993; John Putney, interview, 8 May 2015; and Paul Vaassen, interview.

29. John Putney, interview, 8 May 2015; and Beth Greiner, telephone conversation. See also "Completed Application for Transportation Enhancement Funding, Des Moines Area MPO," 1994, and "Statewide Transportation Enhancement Funding Application, Iowa Department of Transportation," 28 November 1994, both in Beth Greiner Papers.

30. *Des Moines Register*, 15 July, 21 September 1994; 21 June 1995. See also John Putney, interview, 8 May 2015.

31. John Putney, interview, 8 May 2015; Beth Greiner, telephone conversation; and "Treasure Our Fair," video, 24 March 1993, John Putney Papers.

32. Judy Nye, telephone conversation with author, 21 August 2015.

33. Iowa State Fair Blue Ribbon Foundation press release, 19 October 1994, Rox Laird Papers; and *Des Moines Register*, 24 October 1994.

34. *Des Moines Register*, 9 November 1994.

35. *Blue Ribbon* (Winter 1995): 2–3; (Winter 2003): 4; Rox Laird notes, 20 October 1994; and unmarked *Des Moines Register* clipping, 1994, John Putney Papers. See also Bob Schlutz, interview; Paul Vaassen, interview; and *Des Moines Register*, 13 July, 8 August 1995.

36. Discussion of replacing Grandstand with a "shed" and Putney quote from Don Greiman with Jan Cox, *A Blue Ribbon Life: Memories of the Iowa State Fair* (Des Moines: Iowa State Fair Blue Ribbon Foundation, 2012), 42. Estimate for Grandstand repair from *Fair Times* (April 1995): 1, Iowa State Fair newsletter, Kathie Swift Papers, private collection held by Kathie Swift, West Des Moines, Iowa.

37. *Blue Ribbon* (Summer 1995): 1. See also *Fair Times* (April 1995): 1; John Putney, interview, 8 May 2015; and Iowa Legislative Fiscal Bureau, "State Fair Capitals, 17 January 1996, https://www.legis.iowa.gov/docs/publications/IR/833.pdf, accessed on 2 November 2015.

38. For Bunke quote, see *Des Moines Register*, 13 August 1995. See also positive review of "State Fair" in *Chicago Tribune*, 14 August 1995; for *Variety* story and quote, see *Variety*, 11 September 1995.

39. Jan Higgins, interview by author, Pleasant Hill, Iowa, 2 June 2015; Jan Higgins, telephone conversation with author, 5 November 2015; Beth Greiner, telephone conversation; and *Des Moines Register*, 16 August 1990; 29 April 1995.

40. May Fair 95 program, Beth Greiner Papers; John Putney, interview, 8 May 2015; and *Blue Ribbon* (Spring 1996): 1; (Winter 1996): 5.

41. On first interns, see *Blue Ribbon* (Summer 1995): 3.

42. Marion Lucas, telephone conversation with author, 12 May 2015; John Putney interview, 23 October 2015; Emily Putney, interview; Beth Greiner, telephone conversation; and Robin Taylor, correspondence. Heiken quotation and more on water at fair from *Blue Ribbon* (Winter 2014): 40.

43. Ibid.; and Jerry Parkin, interview.

44. *Blue Ribbon* (Fall 1995): 2; (Fall 1996): 3; (Fall 1997): 2; (Fall 1998): 2; and (Winter 2014): 40.

45. On role of volunteers at foundation in general, see John Putney, interview, 8 May 2015; and John Putney, correspondence with author, 29 April 2016. Greiner comment and quotation about volunteers from *Blue Ribbon* (Summer 1997): 1.

46. On 2015 volunteers, see *Blue Ribbon* (Fall 2015): 8; and on Margo Fox, see Amy Miller, interview; press release on Margo Fox being named Iowan of the Day, 31 July 2008, at http://readme.readmedia.com/Margo-Fox-Named-Iowan-of-the-Day/265639, accessed on 4 May 2016; and "My State Fair" stories, at https://www.iowastatefair.org/media/news-releases/iowa-state-fair-seeks-my-state-fair-stories-2/, accessed on 4 May 2016. On Fox being the original volunteer and more about her efforts on behalf of the foundation, see *Blue Ribbon* (Summer 2004): 4.

47. John Putney, interview 8 May 2015; Jerry Parkin, interview; *Blue Ribbon* (Fall 1995): 3; (Spring 1996): 3; and "Limited Edition John Deere 4440" order form, Beth Greiner Papers.

48. John Putney, interview, 8 May 2015; Jerry Parkin interview; Robin Taylor, correspondence with author, 10 November 2015; *Des Moines Register*, 7 July 2009; and *Blue Ribbon* (Spring 2004): 3.

49. *Blue Ribbon* (Winter 1996): 1.
50. John Putney, interview, 23 October 2015; Emily Putney, interview.
51. *Blue Ribbon* (Winter 1996): 1–2.
52. Ibid., 3.
53. *Des Moines Register*, 14 July 1996.
54. Ibid.
55. Ibid.; see also *Des Moines Register*, 15 August 2001.
56. *Blue Ribbon* (Summer 1997): 2; and Beth Greiner, telephone conversation.
57. John Putney, interviews, 8 May, 23 October 2015; Susan Knapp, interview by author, Van Meter, Iowa, 5 October 2012; and Bill Knapp, interview by author, West Des Moines, Iowa, 24 August 2012.
58. John Putney, interview, 8 May 2015.
59. Ibid.; and Bill Knapp, interview, 24 August 2012. For more on gift and Knapp's quotation, see *Des Moines Register*, 12 February 1997.
60. John Putney, interview, 23 October 2015; Emily Putney, interview.
61. Beth Greiner, correspondence with author, 15 December 2015.
62. *Des Moines Register*, 7 August 1997.

CHAPTER 5

1. *Des Moines Register*, 12 August 2007.
2. *Omaha World-Herald*, 1 April 2001.
3. John Putney, interview by author, Gladbrook, Iowa, 23 October 2015.
4. *Blue Ribbon* (Winter 1997): 2; and (Spring 1997): 2, Blue Ribbon Foundation quarterly newsletter, Newsletter Binder, Iowa State Fair Blue Ribbon Foundation Papers, collection held by the Blue Ribbon Foundation, Des Moines, Iowa.
5. John Putney, interview, 23 October 2015; Joyce Lock, telephone conversation with author, 11 December 2015; Beth Greiner, telephone conversation with author, 12 June 2015; Emily Putney, interview by author, Gladbrook, Iowa, 23 October 2015; Dee Wittmack, correspondence with author, 14 December 2015; and *Blue Ribbon* (Spring 1997): 2.
6. Dee Wittmack, correspondence; Joyce Lock, telephone conversation; and Beth Greiner scrapbook, Beth Greiner Papers, private collection held by Beth Greiner, Omaha, Nebraska.

7.   Quotations recalled by both John Putney, interview, 23 July 2015; and Susan Knapp, correspondence with author, 4 December 2015. See also Joyce Lock, telephone conversation.

8.   See Dee Wittmack, correspondence; Joyce Lock, telephone conversation; Beth Greiner, correspondence with author, 15 December 2015; and *Blue Ribbon* (Spring 1997): 3; (Fall 1997): 4; (Summer 1998): 1; and http://www.blueribbonfoundation.org/events/corndog-kickoff, accessed on 15 December 2015; and "A Blue Ribbon Story," commemorative book put together in 2014 by Blue Ribbon Foundation for Putney's retirement, John Putney Papers, private collection held by John Putney, Gladbrook, Iowa [hereafter cited as John Putney Papers]. For quotation, see Susan Knapp, correspondence.

9.   See http://www.blueribbonfoundation.org/events/corndog-kickoff, accessed on 10 December 2016.

10. Beth Greiner, telephone conversation; Marion Lucas, telephone conversation with author, 12 May 2015; Kathie Swift, interview by author, West Des Moines, Iowa, 2 July 2015; and John Putney, interview, 8 May 2015.

11. Marion Lucas, telephone conversation; John Putney, interview, 8 May 2015; and Iowa State Fair Sponsorships brochure, 1997, Beth Greiner scrapbook, Beth Greiner Papers.

12. *Des Moines Register*, 14 August 2001.

13. Beth Greiner, telephone conversation; John Putney, interview, 8 May 2015; Amy Miller, interview, 18 November 2015; Robin Taylor, correspondence with author, 16 November 2015; and *Blue Ribbon* (Spring 1999): 3; (Fall 1999): 6.

14. John Putney, correspondence with author, 25 October 2016.

15. Robin Taylor, interview by author, Des Moines, Iowa, 26 January 2016.

16. See *Blue Ribbon* (Summer 1997): 8; Beth Greiner, telephone conversation.

17. Beth Greiner, telephone conversation; and John Putney, interview, 8 May 2015. For more on Herrig and his quotation, see *Blue Ribbon* (Spring 2014): 6.

18. John Putney, interview, 23 July 2015.

19. John Putney, interview, 8 May 2015.

20. Ibid.

21. Jerry Parkin, interview by author, Winterset, Iowa, 13 October 2015; Susan Knapp, correspondence with author, 4 December 2015.

22. William Friedricks, *The Real Deal: The Life of Bill Knapp* (Des Moines, IA: Business Publications Corp. Inc., 2013), 199–200.

23. John Putney, interviews, 8 May, 23 July 2015; and Kendall Griffith Russell Artiaga, "Iowa State Fair Varied Industries Building, Des Moines Iowa, 23 October 1998, Design Development," Rox Laird Papers, private collection held by Rox Laird, Des Moines, Iowa [hereafter cited as Rox Laird Papers].

24. Scott Worth, interview by author, Des Moines, Iowa, 23 December 2015; and Keffer/Overton Associates, "Varied Industries Building, Iowa State Fairgrounds," Rox Laird Papers.

25. John Putney, interview, 23 October 2015; and Bill Knapp, interview by author, West Des Moines, Iowa, 20 January 2016.

26. *Blue Ribbon* (Summer 1999): 1; and *Des Moines Register*, 25 October 2000.

27. For first quote, see *Des Moines Register*, 25 October 2000; second quote from *Des Moines Register*, 4 December 2000. See also Rox Laird notes, 26 October, 6, 15, 16, November 2000, Rox Laird Papers.

28. On William C. Knapp Varied Industries Building dedication, see *Des Moines Register*, 9 August 2001; and Friedricks, *The Real Deal*, 124. For Lucas on building being a fairgoer favorite, see *Des Moines Register*, 20 August 2001; for quotation about Corndog Kickoff being held in Varied Industries Building for the first time, see *Blue Ribbon* (Winter 2002): 3.

29. Don Greiman with Jane Cox, *A Blue Ribbon Life: Memories of the Iowa State Fair* (Des Moines: Iowa State Fair Blue Ribbon Foundation, 2012), 43–44; and Scott Worth, interview.

30. *Des Moines Register*, 14 August 2002; 2 April 2003.

31. *Blue Ribbon* (Spring 2003): 3; and Greiman, *Blue Ribbon Life*, 44.

32. For first quotation, see *Des Moines Register*, 9 August 1999; for second quotation, see Scott Worth, interview.

33. *Des Moines Register*, 17 July 2000; John Putney, correspondence with author, 5 January 2016; Amy Miller, interview; and Mary Kay Shanley, *Our State Fair: Iowa's Blue Ribbon Story* (Des Moines: Iowa State Fair Blue Ribbon Foundation, 2000).

34. Putney, interview, 8 May 2015; Amy Miller, interview; *Des Moines Register*, 8 August 2001; and Bill Campfield to Rox Laird, 8 August 2007, Rox Laird Papers.

35. John Putney, interview, 8 May 2015.

36. *Des Moines Register*, 3 August 2003. For more on story and context, see Ken Fuson, correspondence with author, 5 January 2016; and John Putney, interview, 23 July 2015.

37. *Des Moines Register*, 3 August 2003.

38. John Putney, interview, 8 May 2015; and *Blue Ribbon* (Winter 2004): 36.

39. Ibid.; and John Putney, correspondence. See also *Des Moines Register*, 26, 27 January, 10 August 2005.

40. John Putney, correspondence; http://www.blueribbonfoundation. org/renovations/museum, and http://www.gftpln.org/Article. do?orgId=6324&articleId=21720, both accessed on 8 January 2016.

41. On Lucas retiring, see *Blue Ribbon* (Winter 2002): 1. For more on this and Huinker quote, see *Des Moines Register*, 24 January 2002.

42. On the Missouri foundation, see http://www.suntimesnews. com/stegen/news/2015/12-December/other/MO%20STATE%20 FAIR%20AUDIT.pdf, accessed on 24 March 2016; for Minnesota State Fair Foundation, see http://www.mnstatefair.org/general_info/ about_us.html, accessed on 12 December 2015; for Kansas State Fairgrounds Foundation, see http://www.fairgroundsfoundation. com/, accessed on 9 January 2016; for Illinois State Fair Museum Foundation, see http://www.statefairmuseum.org/, accessed on 4 January 2016; and for Indiana State Fair Foundation, see Grafton Balko, correspondence with author, 11 January 2016. On Kansas State Fair representatives attending the Corndog Kickoff "to steal ideas," see *Des Moines Register*, 16 July 2006.

43. On Slater, see Gary Slater, interview by author, Des Moines, Iowa, 25 January 2016; http://www.iowafoodandfamily.com/program/ food-thought/conversation-withgary-slater; and http://www. iowastatefair.org/media-center/news-releases/gary-slater-named- 2012-chair-of-international-association, both accessed on 8 January 2016. On Kansas State Fair representatives visiting Corndog Kickoff, see *Des Moines Register*, 16 July 2006.

44. On moving, see Robin Taylor, correspondence with author, 19 November 2015; John Putney, correspondence; Gary Slater, interview; and *Blue Ribbon* (Summer 2002): 4.

45. John Putney, correspondence.

46. Ibid.

47. *Des Moines Register*, 4 August 2002; and *Blue Ribbon* (Summer 2002): 1.

48. Putney correspondence; Sheri Horner, telephone conversation with author, 31 December 2015; and *Blue Ribbon* (Summer 2002): 1, 3.

49. *Des Moines Register*, 8, 13 August 2002; 7 May 2003; *Blue Ribbon* (Summer 2002): 4; (Winter 2010): 40; and Susan Knapp, correspondence.

50. For Slater's statement and quote, see *Des Moines Register*, 6 August 2006; on attendance, see http://www.iowastatefair.org/about-us/trivia/, accessed on 14 January 2016, and https://www.iowastatefair.org/about/fair-dates-attendance/, accessed on 11 December 2016. On master plan, see Scott Worth, interview.

51. Gary Slater, interview; and Paul Vaassen, interview by author, Des Moines, Iowa, 12 August 2015.

52. Shanley, *Our State Fair*, 267; Bob Schlutz, interview by author, Des Moines, Iowa, 17 August 2015; and Scott Worth, interview.

53. John Putney, interview, 10 July 2012; and Bill Knapp, interview by author, West Des Moines, Iowa, 24 August 2012.

54. Ibid.; see also *Des Moines Register*, 6 August 2006. For Paul Knapp Animal Learning Center and Knapp quote, see *Blue Ribbon* (Fall 2006): 3. See also Greiman, *Blue Ribbon Life*, 45.

55. *Des Moines Register*, 5 August 2007. For Laird's comments and quote, see *Des Moines Register*, 12 August 2007.

56. John Putney, interview, 10 July 2012; and Jim Cownie, interview by author, Des Moines, Iowa, 17 September 2012.

57. Ibid.; and Robin Taylor, correspondence, 18 January 2016.

58. John Putney, correspondence; Denny Elwell, interview by author, Ankeny, Iowa, 19 July 2016; and Gary Slater, interview.

59. Ibid.; Bill Knapp, interview; and Greiman, *Blue Ribbon Life*, 47.

60. Emily Putney, interview, 17 August 2015; John Putney, telephone conversation with author, 18 February 2016; and Carly Fisher, correspondence with author, 18 February 2016.

61. John Putney, correspondence. See also *Sioux City Journal*, 29 August 2007; and Scott Worth, interview. For quotation about exhibition center, see "Richard O. Jacobson Exhibition Center at the Iowa State Fair," brochure, n.d., Rox Laird Papers.

62. Emily Putney, interview, 23 October 2015; Bill Knapp, interview, 20 January 2016; and Susan Knapp, interview by author, West Des Moines, Iowa, 20 January 2016.

63. Scott Worth, interview; and John Putney, 23 October 2015.

64. John Putney, interview, 23 October 2015; Rox Laird interview with Robin Taylor, n.d., Rox Laird Papers; and Bill Knapp, interview. Quotation from Scott Worth, interview.

65. Scott Worth, interview; "Agricultural Exhibition Center," Rox Laird Papers.

66. Blue Ribbon Foundation press release, "Richard O. Jacobson Donates $3.5 million to Iowa State Fair," 6 August 2008, Rox Laird Papers.

67. John Putney, correspondence; and Blue Ribbon Foundation press release, "Iowa State Fair receives $1 million contribution for AG Exhibition Center from Iowa businessman Bruce Rastetter," 6 August 2008, Rox Laird Papers.

68. For Susan Knapp quotation, see Susan Knapp, interview; for black box quotation, see Scott Worth, interview; on opening of Jacobson Center, see *Blue Ribbon* (Fall 2010): 1; for description of center, see http://www.blueribbonfoundation.org/renovations/jacobson-center.

69. For crown jewel statement, see Gary Slater, interview; for Greiman's thinking and quotation, see Greiman, *Blue Ribbon Life,* 46, 49; and for World Percheron Congress booking arena before construction was begun, see Paul Vaassen, interview.

70. John Putney, interview, 23 July 2015; Gary Slater, interview; Robin Taylor, interview; and *Blue Ribbon* (Fall 2010): 6.

71. Robin Taylor, interview, and correspondence with author, 19 February 2016.

72. John Putney, interviews, 8 May, 23 October 2015; Gary Slater, interview; and Robin Taylor, interview. For Rox Laird essay and quotation, see *Des Moines Register*, 3 August 2003.

73. For creation of endowment and Putney quote, see *Blue Ribbon* ((Summer 2011): 1; on endowment legislation, see Governor Terry Branstad to Secretary of State of Iowa Matthew Schultz, 11 April 2011, Rox Laird Papers.

74. Gary Slater, interview; and John Putney, interviews, 8 May, 23 July, 2015.

CHAPTER 6

1. *Des Moines Register*, 8 August 2012.

2. *Blue Ribbon* (Spring 2011): 4; (Fall 2012): 6, Blue Ribbon Foundation quarterly newsletter, Newsletter Binder, Iowa State Fair Blue Ribbon Foundation Papers, collection held by Blue Ribbon Foundation, Des Moines, Iowa. For more on Expo Hill project and quotation, see *Des Moines Register*, 8 August 2012.

3. Robin Taylor, interview by author, Des Moines, Iowa, 26 January 2015; and *Blue Ribbon*(Spring 2011): 4.

4. Robin Taylor, interview; John Putney, interview by author, Gladbrook, Iowa, 23 October 2015; telephone conversation with author, 18 February 2016; and Gary Slater, interview by author, Des Moines, Iowa, 25 January 2016.

5. *Des Moines Register*, 16 August 2009.

6. John Putney, interview, 8 May 2015; telephone conversation; Gary Slater, interview; Robin Taylor, interview; Scott Worth, interview by author, Des Moines, Iowa, 23 December 2015.

7. Ibid. For more on stage and quotation, see KCCI Channel 8 news broadcast, 12 August 2015, from video on YouTube, https://www.youtube.com/watch?v=x0UlztvVvSI, accessed on 9 January 2016.

8. John Putney, interviews, 8 May, 23 July 2015. For Ruan in general, see William Friedricks, *In for the Long Haul: The Life of John Ruan* (Ames: Iowa State University Press, 2003).

9. Gary Slater, interview. For background on Ruan's interest in beautification and gardening, see *Des Moines Register*, 16 July 2002; 9 October 2011; and Christine Riccelli, "Where They Lead," *DSM* magazine online, http://www.dsmmagazine.com/botanical-garde/, accessed on 11 February 2016.

10. John Ruan III's quotation from Jerry Parkin, interview by author, Winterset, Iowa, 13 October 2015; John Putney, interview, 23 October 2015.

11. For quotation, see *Des Moines Register*, 22 August 2011; and for general background, see John Putney, telephone conversation.

12. Gary Slater, interview; Scott Worth, interview; John Putney, interview, 23 October 2015. Quotation from http://www.blueribbonfoundation.org/renovations/ruan-plaza, accessed on 15 February 2016.

13. Bob Schlutz, interview by author, Des Moines, Iowa, 17 August 2015; and Jerry Parkin, interview; and Robin Taylor, correspondence with author, 19 February 2016.

14. Jerry Parkin, interview; Scott Worth, interview; and Robin Taylor, correspondence.

15. Sheri Horner, telephone conversation with author, 31 December 2015; John Putney, interview, 8 May 2015; John Putney, correspondence; and *Blue Ribbon* (Summer 2013): 2.

16. Slater quotation from Gary Slater, interview. Elwell quotation from *A Blue Ribbon Story*, commemorative book put together in 2014 by Blue Ribbon Foundation for Putney's retirement, John Putney Papers, private collection held by John Putney, Gladbrook, Iowa [hereafter cited as John Putney Papers].

17. John Putney, interview, 9 July 2016. For start of Fairgrounds 5K Run, see *Blue Ribbon* Fall 2007): 3. Beary left the foundation in 2015 and was replaced by Gina Rooney, who stayed for two years. In 2017, Meg Courter, who had worked in the advancement office at Dowling Catholic High School, took over as the foundation's sponsorship director.

18. John Putney, interview, 23 October 2015; and Emily Putney, interview by author, Gladbrook, Iowa, 23 October 2015.

19. Peter Cownie, interview by author, Des Moines, Iowa, 19 February 2016; and John Putney, interview, 8 May 2015.

20. Ibid. Quotation recounted in Gary Slater, interview.

21. Peter Cownie, interview, 19 February 2016; and Gary Slater, interview. For more on Fair Board meeting and Parkin quote, see John Putney, interview, 23 July 2015.

22. Peter Cownie, interview, 19 February 2016.

23. Ibid.; see also John Putney, interview, 23 October 2015; and *Des Moines Register*, 9 August 2013.

24. Putney quotation from *Blue Ribbon* (Winter 2014): 1.

25. Cownie quotation from *Blue Ribbon* (Fall 2013): 1; see also Peter Cownie, interview, 19 February 2016. On Cownie and Putney, see Robin Taylor, interview; and Gary Slater, interview.

26. John Putney, telephone conversation; and *Blue Ribbon* (Summer 2015): 4.

27. John Putney, telephone conversation; Peter Cownie, interview, 19 February 2016; and Robin Taylor, correspondence, 19 February 2016.

28. Ibid.

29. Robin Taylor, interview.

30. Event and statement recalled by author, who directs the Iowa History Center and hosted Bill and Susan Knapp for lunch at Simpson College to see the statue, 7 March 2014.

31. Author's recollection of events, 7–17 March, 2014; and *Des Moines Register*, 4 April 2014.

32. For Chappell quotation, see *Des Moines Register*, 4 September 2014.

33. Peter Cownie, interview, 19 February 2016.

34. Robin Taylor, interview; Peter Cownie, interview, 18 October 2016.

35. Ibid.

36. Ibid.; and *Des Moines Register*, 28 September 2016.

37. Peter Cownie, interview, 19 February 2016; and correspondence with author, 16 May 2016.

38. Gary Slater, interview.

CONCLUSION

1. "A Proud Iowa Tradition Crumbles in Distress," Iowa State Fair brochure, 1988, Kathie Swift Papers, private collection held by Kathie Swift, West Des Moines, Iowa.

2. Gary Slater, interview by author, Des Moines, Iowa, 25 January 2016. See also "Proud Iowa Tradition Crumbles," and "Treasure Our Fair" campaign brochure 1993, Iowa State Fair Blue Ribbon Foundation, Rox Laird Papers, private collection held by Rox Laird, Des Moines, Iowa.

3. Paul Vaassen, interview by author, Des Moines, Iowa, 12 August 2015; and John Putney, interview by author, Des Moines, Iowa, 10 July 2012.

4. Slater quotation from *A Blue Ribbon Story*, commemorative book put together in 2014 by Blue Ribbon Foundation for Putney's retirement, John Putney Papers, private collection held by John Putney, Gladbrook, Iowa.

5. *Des Moines Register*, 3 August 2003.

6. Don Greiman with Jane Cox, *A Blue Ribbon Life: Memories of the Iowa State Fair* (Des Moines, IA: The Blue Ribbon Foundation, 2012), 48–9.

7. Beth Greiner, correspondence with author, 15 June 2015.

8. Cownie quoted in *Blue Ribbon* (Fall 2013): 1, Blue Ribbon Foundation's quarterly newsletter, Newsletter Binder, Iowa State Fair Blue Ribbon Foundation Papers, collection held by the Blue Ribbon Foundation, Des Moines, Iowa.

9. Cownie's first quote from Peter Cownie, interview by author, Des Moines, Iowa, 19 February 2016; second quotation from *Blue Ribbon* (Winter 2016): 1.

10. Jan Higgins, interview by author, Pleasant Hill, Iowa, 2 June 2015.

11. Jerry Parkin, interview by author, Winterset, Iowa, 13 October 2015.

12. Quotation from *Des Moines Register*, 9 August 2001.

INDEX

Made in the USA
Columbia, SC
04 August 2017